NAVIGATING
INTEGRITY

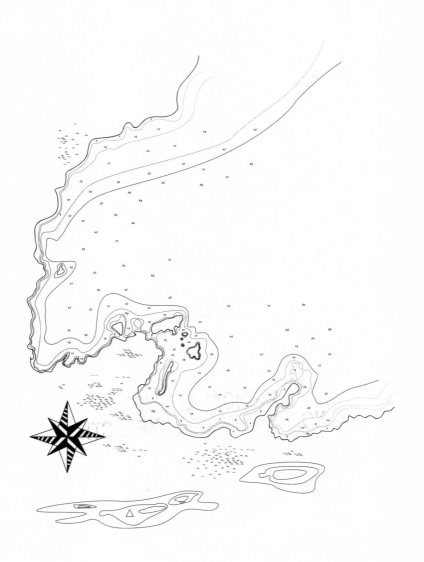

To Larry
Best wishes
navigating integrity !
Al

NAVIGATING INTEGRITY

TRANSFORMING BUSINESS *AS USUAL* INTO BUSINESS *AT ITS BEST*

AL WATTS

inTEgro, Inc.
www.integro-inc.com

BRIO PRESS
12 South Sixth Street # 1250
Minneapolis, MN 55402

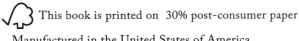 This book is printed on 30% post-consumer paper

Manufactured in the United States of America
10 9 8 7 6 5 4 3 2 1

Brio Press is a division of Brio Books.
Book Artwork and Design by Anthony Sclavi
Edited by Victoria Miller
Photography Licensed from istockphoto.com

Library of Congress Control Number: 2010936139
    Watts, Al.
    Navigating Integrity/Al Watts
    ISBN 13: 978-0-9826687-4-0 (paper)
    1. Business 2. Management

This book is dedicated to all who never lost faith that I would live up to my promise, principally Carley, Alison, Kristin, Mom and Dad, and to the memory of Margaret Poseley, who in her life and work modeled what this book is about.

Ten percent of proceeds from the sale of this book will be donated to the P&G Children's Safe Drinking Water Fund through The Greater Cincinnati Foundation. (www.csdw.org)

Every day more than 4,000 children in developing countries die from lack of potable water, more than from HIV/AIDS and malaria combined. Your book purchase will provide one child in a developing country with at least a month's supply of clean drinking water.

Thank you.

Please visit www.csdw.org to learn more about how your donation will be put to work.

ACKNOWLEDGEMENTS

Indeed we all stand on the shoulders of giants, and as the jazz great Sonny Criss put it: "I listen to everybody . . . Everybody takes from everybody else and adds their own thing and goes on from there." First I am grateful for all the "giants" that I have learned from; many of them are referenced here, including Warren Bennis, James Collins, Stephen Covey (father and son), Howard Gardner, Robert Greenleaf and Parker Palmer. Closer to home, I am grateful for the association, coaching and friendship of Kevin Cashman, Richard Leider, Doug Lennick and Jim Mitchell – all of whom I always viewed as comrades pursuing the transformation of "business as usual" into business at its best.

I wish to also thank all of my clients – you know who you are – for giving me the opportunity to help you be the best that you can be while learning the lessons that culminated in this book. Thanks, too, to my consulting partners over the years for all that you have contributed to our clients' and to my growth.

It is one thing to write a book, and another thing entirely to publish one that gets into readers' hands with the desired effect. A big "thank you" to my editor Tori Miller, designer Anthony Sclavi, publicist Sara Lien and their talented team at Brio Books. Thanks too to Margie Adler, Kent Garborg, Steve Wilbers, friends and associates for the generous advice and support that you offered from the beginning; without it I would still just have a "book in me."

Above all, thanks to Carley and our girls, Alison and Kristin, my main support and the inspiration for doing what I do every day and for trying to be my best.

CONTENTS

Seeing the bigger picture
Truth-telling
Transparency
Authenticity means action.

INTRODUCTION

After nearly thirty years as a consultant to all manner of organizations and their leaders – some that had great success, some that failed and many in between, I've come to the conclusion that *integrity* is mainly what differentiated them. This book goes beyond integrity as we are used to hearing about it – a moral or ethical virtue, although that is certainly part of the picture. "Being of sound moral principle; uprightness, honesty and sincerity" is only one of Webster's[1] definitions of integrity, and yes, especially on the heels of our worst economic meltdown since the Great Depression, we likely need few reminders of the need to integrate *"sound moral principles, uprightness, honesty and sincerity"* into the DNA of our leaders and organizations.

Webster's first and second definitions of integrity are about being "unbroken," "whole," "unimpaired" and "sound," all of which speak more to matters of leadership and organizational effectiveness. Exceptional leaders and organizations in the twenty-first century – those who live up to their *whole* promise – the best that they can be – will be those that embody all of these dimensions. They will be the leaders and organizations that model what Howard Gardner[2] calls "good work" – *effective, engaging* and *ethical* – the "triple-e" leaders and organizations that we aspire to associate with.

Doing well in the market place, doing good (or at least no harm,) engaging work and meaningful lives are not independent, but integrated challenges. Leaders and organizations that simultaneously meet those challenges, integrating effectiveness with ethics and value with values, will be the ones that transform our institutions from "business as usual" to business at its best. This book is for those aspiring to be that kind of leader and to lead that kind of organization.

We will talk more in Chapter Two about the importance for leaders and organizations of knowing their "stories." Here are three of mine leading me to conclude that integrity is central to what it will take for leaders and organizations to transform business as usual into business at its best:

INTEGRITY – BRIDGING VALUE AND VALUES

First a recollection from my college days: I still remember the long walks across the river that separated the business school from the rest of my college campus. The distance between campuses and the river that divided them turned out to be more symbolic than I knew at the time, and prophetic of the drive in most of my professional life to bridge gaps and to unify.

College for me was in the late 1960s and early 1970s – at the rise of efforts to be more socially conscious and environmentally aware. There were almost daily opportunities then to dodge class and participate in protests about the Vietnam War, genocide, race relations or "the military industrial complex." While many of my liberal arts friends and that campus in general were engaged in those pursuits, one would hardly know on the business campus ("training ground for the military industrial complex!") what all the fuss was about. At that time in business school it was easy to get the message that environmental issues, peace, race relations, the arts and humanities were peripheral issues that had little to do with "the bottom line." Those were the days when the literal divide between business and business at its best first began to sink in for me, just as the distance and river dividing my university campuses separated the business school from the rest of what was worth paying attention to.

That boundary-spanning experience in college evolved into a career in human resources management and organization development – opportunities to connect the people side of organizations with the business of those organizations. Thirty years later, however, it seems that for many there is still a divide between who they are and who they are at work, just like the disconnect between the business and liberal arts campuses at my alma mater. We are still in need of a bridge between what will be required to make the next quarter's numbers and what it takes to be a sustainable organization and good community citizen; there is still a separation between affairs of business, or "the bottom line" – *value* – and what sustains human hearts and spirits – *values*.

INTEGRITY – BRIDGING *ETHICS* WITH *EFFECTIVENESS*

My second story picks up at the end of my Human Resources career "on the inside," when I had the opportunity to witness first-hand the unraveling of a once promising technology company. It made some typical mistakes for a rapidly growing start-up that it could have recovered from. Its greatest misstep, however, was misreporting revenue, which coupled with a few other ethically questionable practices, led to its demise. It was sad of course that many (including me) lost their jobs and that investors (including me) lost a lot of money. Most unfortunate was that the company really had terrific products and terrific talent, but would never recover or fulfill the promise it once had. That was an early and vivid experience that helped me realize that living up to our potential as leaders and organizations requires attention to effectiveness <u>and</u> ethics – to doing things right and doing the right things.

INTEGRITY – PULLING IT ALL TOGETHER

My third story finds me again on a bridge spanning a river. After ten years in industry then fifteen years as the founder and partner in an organization effectiveness consulting practice, I was reflecting on my life purpose as part of an executive development retreat. I was restless and open to a change, driven partly by a heavy travel schedule and our youngest daughter's chronic illness, which contributed to feelings of life and work being out of sync. I also longed for more work where as William James put it "I felt deeply and intensely active and alive . . . when a voice inside speaks and says 'this is the real me.'"

Ultimately I sold my shares back to my partners in the firm that I started fifteen years earlier and refocused my consulting practice by asking these questions: *What leaders and organizations did I know that were simultaneously effective, engaging and ethical? Which not only thrived as commercial entities but earned reputations as great places to work and model community citizens?* Those would be the leaders and organizations that best connected value with values, effectiveness with ethics and who we are with who we are at work; those would be the leaders and organizations most capable of living up to their promise and transforming business as usual to business at its best.

Those leaders and organizations – the ones that model the kind of integrity that this book is about – successfully navigate four critical challenges:

THE IDENTITY CHALLENGE: Organizations and leaders that master the *Identity* challenge know who they are and where they are going. They have a strong sense of purpose that they articulate along with their values and aims in ways that engage followers. They have a distinct identity and strategies for creating value while, as Stephen Young[3] defines "moral capitalism," "asserting self-interest toward the whole." They fully inhabit their strengths and know their limitations.

Think of leaders and organizations you know that excel and others that fall short of their promise; no doubt one differentiator is the degree that those leaders and organizations are clear about who they are, what they stand for, their strengths and their limitations. Contrast that with many institutional failures contributing to the 2008 economic meltdown that demonstrated mission and values drift – financial institutions with missions to preserve wealth that operated more like casinos, and regulatory agencies that fell short of their mission to regulate and protect public interests. Surely you are also acquainted with leaders and organizations that failed on account of not fully inhabiting their strengths or on account of their blind spots.

THE AUTHENTICITY CHALLENGE is mostly about *trueness* – to mission, values and aims, *truth* – facing and articulating reality, and *transparency*. Opaque balance sheets, suspect financial transactions and decisions linked to some of the latest institutional and leadership failures were certainly ethically flawed. In line with this book's argument, however, that lack of transparency likely had as much to do with impairing engagement and effectiveness as it did with ethics.

Authentic leaders and authentic organizations create truth-telling cultures; they "call them as they see them" and encourage others to do the same, knowing that the perspectives of many add up to better decisions and courses of action. Think of the damage done in organizations or by leaders you've known due to hedging or concealment of the truth, misrepresentation or simply not being aware of what was going on; if nothing else we have only to reflect on less than candid performance appraisals and their effect on careers or productivity. What do you think the dividend would be in your organization if somehow truth-telling improved by just ten percent? How about fifty percent?

There is a sense of coherence, or harmony, in the lives of leaders and in organizations that master the ALIGNMENT CHALLENGE. To paraphrase Warren Bennis, they appear as "tapestries of intention," where what we see and what we experience are one with who or what they profess to be. Who and how they hire, train and reward send signals that reinforce their purpose, values and aims; the left hand does not undo what the right hand is doing.

Aligned leaders and organizations are constantly adapting and learning – or realigning, so their views of reality and actions square with their markets and environments. They are firm around core values and aims, but flexible about everything else; they not only "walk the talk," but "dance the dance." As Margaret Fuller, an early equal rights proponent and friend of Ralph Waldo Emerson, said: "Harmony exists in difference no less than likeness, if only the same key note governs both parts." Aligned leaders and organizations balance the requirements of unity, or agreement around the "same key note," with diversity – of opinions, perspectives and points of view.

Mastering the ACCOUNTABILITY CHALLENGE means taking responsibility and delivering on our promises – whether brand promises, goals we set or commitments we make; to live up to our promise and potential we need to fulfill all of these. Truly accountable organizations and leaders keep track of what matters and count what counts – not just financial or short-term results. They exercise real stewardship of not only resources under their direct control, but for consequences of their decisions and actions however far away.

As I first learned from Larry Wilson, founder of Pecos River Learning and Wilson Learning, "a map is not the territory," but the model that follows illustrates some overall themes: *Identity*, the first integrity challenge and first dimension of this *Leadership And Organizational Integrity Model*, appears at the base since it is foundational; if we don't know who we are, where we stand or what we want to accomplish, much of the rest doesn't matter. When we know who we are, what we believe and what we intend to accomplish, the model's second dimension, *Authenticity* – speaking our truth and being what we say we are, logically follows. *Alignment* is near the middle because integrity often requires mediation – as in mediating our aims with external realities or achieving unity amidst diversity. The model's last dimension, *Accountability*, appears last from bottom to top to reflect that living up to our promise – be it keeping a brand promise or more broadly, achieving our potential, is largely driven by successfully navigating the earlier challenges.

Since ancient history, a triangle has symbolized variations of unity, wholeness, harmony and synthesis – much of what integrity helps us accomplish, and therefore seems an apt background. "Organization," "Leader" and "Team" appear as their own separate triangles within the larger triangle to reflect that in real life they stand alone as well. An ongoing challenge and opportunity, particularly for leaders, is paying attention not only to the alignment or integration of their own values and aspirations with those of their organization, but also to the alignment of their team and team members' values and aspirations with those of the organization.

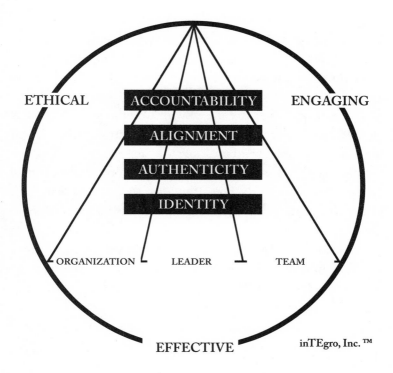

Early on I was asked if this book is intended for leaders or to improve organizational effectiveness; my answer is "yes," or both. I am a sailor, so you will find sailing analogies throughout here. In that vein, let me elaborate on my "both" response. I could no more easily separate a vessel from her captain when judging fitness for sea than I can separate organizations from their leaders when evaluating their effectiveness and sustainability. Reaching a destination at sea without undue stress on vessel or crew requires both a seaworthy vessel and a fit captain. Likewise, transforming "business as usual" into business at its best requires that both organizations and their leaders be suited for the journey.

This book is an interactive guide first to help leaders successfully navigate the four integrity challenges. My hope is that leaders can then use insights that they gain and the tools here to help their organizations be the best they can be by meeting those same challenges.

Chapter One sets the stage by making the "case" for integrity – the business case as well as its connection to health and wellness, desirable attributes of leaders, trust, engagement, change management and growth. Chapters Two through Five address the *Identity, Authenticity, Alignment* and *Accountability* challenges respectively, including applications for leaders and their organizations.

Not all of the concepts here will be new; some we may know but have difficulty applying. That's where Chapter Six comes in, a guide for developing six critical leadership and organizational capabilities to more effectively navigate the integrity challenges: three "Cs" – *Competency, Consistency* and *Courage,* and three "Ds" – *Discipline, Discernment* and *Dialog.*

Questions throughout each chapter will help you apply the tools here to your life, work and organization. While each chapter is a relatively quick read, responding authentically to some of the questions may take you considerably longer, and in some cases you are encouraged to seek others' input and opinions. Executives, managers and team leaders will likely find the questions with organizational applications useful for conversation with those you work with. By taking the time for thoughtfully responding to the questions, you should be well on your way to increasing your and your organization's capability for navigating integrity challenges.

Readers are also invited to use the pass code on page 171 for accessing inTEgro's online *Leadership Integrity Survey.* Your report will give you a fix on how you are currently navigating integrity challenges, along with suggestions for closing integrity gaps.

Each of us is born as a promise, and each of the communities we form comes into existence as a promise; fundamentally, integrity is about living up to that promise and becoming the best that we can be. May the pages that follow serve as a catalyst for you and your organization to live up to your promise and be among those who are transforming business as usual into business at its best.

CHAPTER 1 | *INTEGRITY MATTERS*

As I see it now, leadership is character, and the process of becoming a leader is much the same as becoming an integrated human being.
Warren Bennis

Integrity is one of several paths. It distinguishes itself from the others because it is the right path, and the only one upon which you will never get lost.
M. H. McKee

The leader for today and the future will be focused on how to be — how to develop quality, character, mind-set, values, principles and courage.
Frances Hesselbein

ETHICS AND THE BUSINESS CASE

Since the usual and typical first definition of integrity is about ethics, we will begin there. It's also a good place to start since Webster's[1] third definition of "integrity" – "sound moral principles, uprightness and honesty" – seems to be on our minds a lot these days given the news. I started writing this book during the classic Enron shenanigans, which conservatively led to direct losses in the billions of dollars. Arthur Andersen, Enron's auditor, was tied in with the whole mess, which effectively put that eighty-plus-year-old once venerable practice out of business. A 2002 boston.com study estimated that Enron-related losses cost American taxpayers over $200 billion dollars in lost savings, jobs, pensions and tax revenue alone; the ripple effects, counting personal bankruptcies, health impact, uncollectible loans, etc. are almost incalculable. Shoot ahead about eight years and we have the Bernie Madoff case, the private investment counselor who "made off" with an estimated

> *Integrity is the cornerstone of free enterprise, and all leaders need a clear teachable point of view on it.*
> Noel Tichy

fifty billion of investors' and foundations' dollars in a giant Ponzi scheme. I could go on and on – you read the headlines too; the monetary costs of ethical lapses in the last ten years alone would likely be sufficient to erase our national debt!

Not only can lacking that kind of integrity be expensive, but demonstrating it apparently pays dividends. Walker Information research[2] has consistently shown that integrity ranks just below employee treatment as a factor that influences where people choose to work and employee loyalty; their research also shows strong correlations between employee loyalty and customer loyalty. Three fourths of Walker respondents in one study cited a poor reputation for ethics as the second most influential factor guiding their decision not to buy something, behind only service. Winning the admiration of employees and the trust of customers translates to increased loyalty. That translates to reduced turnover and recruiting costs, stronger brands and reduced selling costs, which improve bottom lines.

> *Whether you're on a sports team, in an office or a member of a family, if you can't trust one another there's going to be trouble.*
> Joe Paterno

INTEGRITY – THE FOUNDATION FOR TRUST

Trust is the basic capital of our economy and is driven for the most part by the integrity of our institutions and leaders. Warren Bennis[3] believes that "Integrity is the basis of trust, which is not as much an ingredient of leadership as it is a product." Without trust, there would be no investors, customers would not buy our products or services, it would be hard to recruit workers and harder to retain them. The credit and financial market crisis that gained momentum in 2008 was fed by lack of trust and fear that money lent may not be paid back. Trust is required for cooperative work relationships and for the formation of partnerships and alliances that are crucial in our economy. Without trusting that old ways can be set aside and that new strategies can work, executing real change in organizations would be nearly impossible.

WHOM DO YOU TRUST?

If integrity is the basis of trust as Bennis suggests, what is it about integrity that contributes to trust? We trust leaders and organizations that are clear about their goals and what they stand for – *Identity*. We trust leaders and organizations that are true to their goals and values, and that model truth-telling and transparency – *Authenticity*. We trust leaders and organizations with the capacity to create unity around shared goals – *Alignment*, and we trust leaders and organizations that deliver as promised and take responsibility for their decisions and actions – *Accountability*.

What dividends do you think you and your organization would reap if improving *Identity, Authenticity, Alignment* and *Accountability* increased trust levels by ten percent? What about twenty percent? How about if they doubled?

"DIVIDED WE FALL"

Although an infrequent descriptor of effective leadership and organizations, *wholeness* – Webster's first definition of "integrity," is an apt one. Lack of wholeness – dividedness, manifests itself when we accept behavior or values on the job that we would find unacceptable in our personal lives, justifying it by thinking that "it's just business." It manifests itself when what we do day in and day out does not resonate with any sense of purpose or call on our best gifts and talents. It manifests itself when we question the value of our products or services or believe they may even be harmful, rationalizing that "it's just a living," or that "if we didn't provide it, someone else would." It manifests itself when on Sunday night or Monday morning we are sick at heart about the prospect of another day in the office or at the plant.

> *Be really whole and all things will come to you.*
> Lao-Tzu

A recent Gallup[4] survey showed that only 29% of American workers said they were "engaged" – feeling loyal and productive, 56% were "not engaged" – just putting in time, and 15% were "actively disengaged" – unhappy and spreading their discontent. The National Institute of Mental Health estimates that untreated depression and mental health issues at work cost employers about $44 billion annually. It's no stretch to conclude that feeling disconnected between who we are and who we are at work contributes significantly to disengagement and depression.

> *Meaninglessness inhabits the fullness of life and can, therefore, be equated with illness; meaningfulness makes a great many things endurable, perhaps everything.*
> Carl Jung

This disconnect between work and the rest of our lives has not always been so pronounced. In early Christian times, life to Saint Benedict meant *ora et labora* – "to pray and to work." "Vocation," from the Latin *vocare*, or "calling," was viewed as a calling from God, and Martin Luther believed that everyone's vocation was sacred. According to Luther, salvation was a function of belief in God and performing the tasks that were required of one's station. It was John Calvin's extension of Luther's beliefs that planted the seeds for what C. Michael Thompson[5] describes as "The Great Divorce" between life and work. Reformed ministers who preached Calvin's message claimed that one's vocational success was a reflection of the grace granted by God – as measured by the material gain from one's work.

> To be yourself in a world that is constantly trying to make you something else is the greatest accomplishment.
> Ralph Waldo Emerson

As the Enlightenment caught on and secularized this "Puritan work ethic," material gain soon came to be viewed as a worthwhile end in itself. This split between work and life gained momentum with the Industrial Revolution in the eighteenth century. Before that, in agrarian and craft economies worker and product were more closely bound; farmers and craft workers were more involved in all stages of production and could identify more with the end product. During the Industrial Revolution people left their homes to work at times set by others, in large facilities and with tools they did not own; they performed specialized repetitive tasks that contributed only partially to a finished product that they never saw and that was likely not used in their immediate community.

We've come a long way since the Industrial Revolution, but the schism between work and who we are is still present for many.

Integrity as wholeness means closing divides between our work and the rest of our lives and healing the "working wounded." The payoff includes higher quality-of-life, greater engagement, increased effectiveness, improved health and lower costs.

INTEGRITY AND HARMONY

If integrity is about wholeness and completeness, it can bridge other kinds of divides as well. Examples include lack of alignment around organizational goals or values, and individuals or teams working at cross-purposes – typical scenarios when I'm asked by clients to "get everyone on the same page." How much easier and energizing would work be, how many resources would be conserved, and how much better would results be if we could only increase alignment around organizational goals? When I ask clients how much energy they think is being wasted in their organizations on account of these kinds of disconnects, estimates range from twenty to eighty percent! How much more effective and profitable would our organizations be, and how much more fulfilling

> *An organization that is at war with itself will not have the strength or focus to survive and thrive in today's competitive environment.*
> Prof. John O. Whitney

would work be, if all of that energy could be channeled in the same direction? Proficiency navigating the *Alignment* challenge will help us close those kinds of gaps and disconnects.

INTEGRITY AND THE LEADERSHIP MIND.

Integrity is a way of knowing and thinking that is especially critical in complex, rapidly changing environments. Executives in particular need the capacity to see the whole ("big picture") – to recognize interdependencies and the wider concentric circles of stakeholders surrounding their organizations. Leaders and teams with this capacity are able to integrate differences and disparate concepts, recognizing that synthesis can lead to better and more sustainable solutions – a capacity for thinking in terms of "both / and" instead of "either / or." It is a skill critical not only for organizational problem solving, but for building relationships and communities at any level, especially in a world that seems to be shrinking and increasingly fragmented.

The ability of a first rate intelligence is the ability to hold two opposing ideas in the mind at the same time and still retain the ability to function.
F. Scott Fitzgerald

According to David Kolb[6]: "The process of advanced professional work is holistic, involving more synthesis than analysis . . . Less time is spent solving problems and more is spent selecting which problems should be solved, through agenda setting and priority setting. . . Integrity is an epistemic concept describing the highest form of human intelligence . . . a normative ideal describing the kind of knowing process we humans value most highly, the process of human judgment that we choose to rely on to create our collective future." This is the kind of integrative mindset needed for not only doing things right, but determining the right things to do, and for creating unity with diversity.

Selecting and developing talent with this kind of mindset pays dividends in the form of a more strategic orientation, better long-term decisions, community building and sustainability.

Wit lies in recognizing the resemblance among things which differ, and the difference between things that are alike.
Madame DeStael

INTEGRITY AND CHANGE MANAGEMENT

In 1994 Jim Collins[7] and Jerry Porras published their research confirming what I had suspected after many years as a consultant: organizations with enduring *Core Ideologies* – their mission and core values for the most part – deliver considerably higher returns than those without them. In their research Collins and Porras identified eighteen fifty-year-old-plus organizations where returns on investments in those organizations were on average six times higher than returns from a group of matched control companies, and twelve times higher than dollars invested in the general stock market. Part of what distinguished those companies that earned substantially higher returns was dogged adherence to their core ideology. Those companies also demonstrated remarkable resiliency and the ability to bounce back from adversity over time. All of the organizations studied, to be thriving after fifty years or more, obviously had devised and executed effective strategies and managed change pretty well. The exceptional companies, however – those creating the greatest sustainable value and demonstrating the highest resiliency, were the ones that were clear about what they were and what they valued – what was not going to change – and stayed true to that, even at a cost. That is the kind of integrity that this book is about.

We are living in a period of incredible, chaotic and disruptive changes technologically, economically, geopolitically and socially; sometimes it's a struggle to just adapt, let alone to get ahead of the game. For the executives I work with, "change management" or some variation of it is usually near the top of their agendas or wish list of organizational capabilities. In addition to questions of what changes to make and how to build capabilities for changing, as Collins and Porras demonstrated effective change management also requires knowing what <u>not</u> to change. These same ideas apply to individuals and teams; we are more resilient and make stronger contributions when we know who we are, who we are not and what we value most, and when we are clear about where to compromise or adapt and when not to.

I love to sail, and am often struck by the wonderful lessons that sailing offers about leadership and organizations. When I learned to sail larger sailboats, I (and especially my wife) were delighted to discover that as long as their hulls maintain structural integrity sailboats right themselves if overturned – a function primarily of their heavy, lead-filled keels and low centers of gravity. That is a perfect analogy for a core ideology – the foundation, or force, keeping us generally headed in the right direction and assuring that we can always recover, even in turbulent seas.

INTEGRITY AND GROWTH

Carl Jung[8], the famous Swiss psychoanalyst, believed that becoming an *integral* human being – all that we can be, is a life-long process of *Individuation* that requires owning all of who we are – strengths and limitations. Surviving and thriving in the years ahead will require integral organizations as well as integral leaders; we have probably all witnessed leaders and organizations that failed on account of either not fully inhabiting their strengths or succumbing to blind spots.

The maxim "grow or die" is true; if leaders and organizations are unable to discard what no longer serves them and to develop new capacities they will likely not survive, let alone thrive. Doing that so we can live up to our promise and be our best requires the kind of fearless self-assessment covered in the next chapter on *Identity*.

SO WHY DOES INTEGRITY MATTER?

Integrity has always been at the foundation of ethical business practices and right living, and evidence of the payoffs abounds. Meeting the four integrity challenges – *Identity, Authenticity, Alignment* and *Accountability* will help us not only fashion ethical lives and organizational cultures, but also reach our potential as effective and engaging leaders and organizations. Mastering the four integrity challenges can be the catalyst for transforming from "business as usual" into business at its best.

We are experiencing a crisis of confidence and trust around the world; those who can best navigate the waters ahead will have a clear sense of who they are – their purpose, their values, their aims, their strengths and their limitations. They will be authentic – true to their purpose and values and displaying the capacity to tell the truth as they see it and help others do the same. They will master alignment challenges and possess the ability to create unity with diversity, reinforce what's most important, grow and adapt. And they will model accountability – delivering on their promises, counting what really counts, and modeling stewardship. These are the kind of leaders that we will follow, the kind of organizations that we will want to be part of, the kind that customers will want to buy from and the kind that communities will support.

> *If you have integrity, nothing else matters. If you don't have integrity, nothing else matters.*
>
> Alan Simpson

CHAPTER 2 | *IDENTITY*

*I have a key in my bosom called Promise,
that will, I am persuaded, open any lock in
Doubting Castle.*
The Pilgrim's Progress

*Purpose is crucial
for all truly great
enterprises. Let
others play with
'strategy,' 'tactics'
and 'management.'
Purpose is the game
of champions.*
Nikos Mourkogiannis

*One must know oneself.
If it does not serve to
discover the truth, it at
least serves as a rule of life
and there is nothing better.*
Blaise Pascal

I like the story about a priest who was stopped by a military sentry. Before letting the priest pass, the sentry asked him three questions: *"Who are you?"*. . . *"What is your business?"* . . . and *"Where are you going?"* After answering the sentry's questions, the priest asked him what he was paid, then said: "My son, if I could I would gladly pay you double that if you meet me here each week and ask me the same questions!"

We could all use someone or the discipline to ask ourselves those questions periodically. To master the *Identity* Challenge and to survive and thrive in the years ahead, our leaders and organizations will need to be crystal clear about who they are – their mission, values and aims, as well as their strengths and "shadow sides." Many of the organizations that failed amidst market troubles that accelerated in 2008 were either muddled about what their missions were or somehow lost their way. Prime examples include banks drifting from their fundamental purpose of providing financial security to pursue risky investments and score quick profits, and regulatory agencies forgetting that their mission was to regulate and provide accountable oversight.

> *The most difficult thing in life is to know yourself.*
>
> Thales

Others that failed the *Identity* challenge included organizations blind to critical flaws or "shadow sides" of their cultures, including cultures that suppressed bad news or disagreement, "too big or proud to fail" cultures, and cultures prone to excessive risk-taking. Often those organizational vulnerabilities were compounded by leaders at high levels with their own blind sides that sealed their fates.

There's a saying that "the sea will uncover weaknesses and exploit them." In a similar vein, market turbulence ahead will be unforgiving of leaders and organizations with muddled missions, character and culture flaws that go unnoticed or leaders and organizations that can't articulate what they stand for. Organizations and leaders alike want workers who are enrolled in their mission and values. Most of us seek work where we feel engaged and where an organization's values resonate with our own. None of that happens unless both organizations and individuals are clear about who they are, what they stand for and what they hope to accomplish.

Fundamental to mastering the *Identity* challenge are three realities: First, we are not alone. As Cicero[1] stated it in *De Officiis:* You must understand that "nature has clothed us, as it were, with two characters. One of them is universal . . . The other is the character bestowed separately on each individual." We are social beings, and our organizations are social institutions; living up to our promise and potential in that context means understanding that we are integrally connected to the larger community and world. Realization of our "universal character" or identity implies a responsibility to consider the impact of our and our organizations' actions on larger and larger concentric rings of "other."

> One need ask only 'What for? What am I to unify my being for?' The reply is: Not for my own sake.
>
> Martin Buber

The second reality is that we are "humans being" before "humans doing;" we are far more than whatever functional roles we play. In the West and developed nations, we tend to identify most with our professional or "doing" roles, making our "homo economicus" identity the scale that we most often measure ourselves by.

Third, there are multiple dimensions of our *beingness*: – our physical, mental, emotional and spiritual selves – that are all connected. Again, especially in the West, we tend to overemphasize the mental and physical dimensions of who we are; if we are not able to figure something out, objectify it or see, taste or touch it, we tend to discount or ignore it.

Since organizations are populated with human beings, the same dimensions – physical, mental, emotional and spiritual are all present there; we ignore or discount any of them at our peril. Carrying on without awareness or respect for all dimensions of our being is like pulling up the proverbial two-legged stool:

results and our satisfaction will be less than what we hoped (and we may be setting ourselves up for a fall!). Many of the heated discussions that I am part of, for example, revolve around organizational direction, structure or decision-making. On the surface they are objective discussions about physical assets dominated by rational arguments. The intensity and tone of discussions at times, however, suggest underlying emotions – perhaps fear, anger, frustration or sadness. An inability or lack of courage to acknowledge and grapple with those emotional dimensions and realities at appropriate times will likely overlook root issues and lead to half-baked solutions.

> *What can we gain by sailing to the moon if we are not able to cross the abyss that separates us from ourselves? This is the most important of all voyages of discovery, and without it, all the others are not only useless, but disastrous.*
> Thomas Merton

Extraordinary results and extraordinary commitment are products of work and interactions that engage all of who we are – body, mind emotions and spirit. Damage done from work that abuses the body is probably easiest to see and understand. Sometimes, however, it is abuse leaving no visible marks that over time inflicts the most damage. Work that dulls our senses, does not fully engage our mental faculties or leaves us spiritually hungry – with little sense of meaning or of making a contribution – leaves us far short of the best outcomes.

In the Introduction I spoke of the need to know both a vessel and her captain to assess our chances of reaching a desired port; we need to know "what they're made of." As we encounter increasingly challenging seas ahead, the same logic applies. In that spirit, this chapter and those that follow will explore how both "captains" (leaders) and their "ships" (organizations) can navigate the four integrity challenges. Stephen Covey's[2] logic of "private before public victories" applies here; most sections begin with applications for leaders since leaders can then be better prepared to ready their "vessels" for what lies ahead.

HOW DO WE KNOW WHO WE ARE?
OUR "STORY"

We all have a "story." As Robert Fulford[3] put it in The Triumph of Narrative: "To discover we have no story is to acknowledge that our existence is meaningless, which we may find unbearable." That story is made up of experiences and memories, each of them a thread, in the tapestry that becomes who we are. Each experience or memory on its own, like a single thread in a tapestry, does not tell the whole story. Looking at a tapestry "whole cloth," however, a pattern emerges.

In his book Crossing The Unknown Sea, David Whyte[4] tells us about the poet Wordsworth's trust in deep physical memory, often from childhood, as clues to how we became who we are: "To a child, the world is a beckoning horizon, and as Wordsworth said 'The Child is the Father of the Man' (and we might add today *Mother of the Woman*.) Whatever particular horizons drew us as a child are the original patterns and templates of our adult belonging." In The Soul's Code, James Hillman[5] relays example after example, from Rommel the WWII "Desert Fox" to Mohandas Gandhi, where early life experiences, childhood obsessions and in some cases traumas "made sense" when looking at their lives backwards. Experiences in their early childhood were the threads

> *To be a person, you have to have a story to tell.*
>
> Isak Dinesen

that, although the pattern did not become visible until later in life, began weaving the tapestry that revealed who they would become.

Knowing our "story" provides one set of clues about who we are. My story begins with my father, a WWII vet, meeting my French mother-to-be when his unit marched through Rheims. After Dad's discharge and my older brother's birth in Paris, Dad brought Mom back to rural Excelsior, Minnesota, which you can imagine was quite a culture shock for her. For as much of my childhood as I can remember, my identity was influenced by a "bi-cultural" state and perspective; I grew up knowing about differences in customs, traditions and values, and how they influence perceptions. That grounding, and knowing that different cultures and points of view can clash but also contribute value, has served me well in my work. It helps me help clients bridge the divide that sometimes exists between different cultures in their organizations – including not just geo-political or cultural divides, but divides like those between physicians and administrators in health care, or between faculty and administrators in educational settings.

> *Each of us needs an adequate biography: How do I put together into a coherent image the pieces of my life? How do I find the basic plot of my story?*
> James Hillman

I also have vivid memories of another thread in the "Al tapestry": our family's first vacation when I was nine years old – a long drive to Michigan to visit friends. We arrived in Sault St. Marie after dark and stopped at the locks where ships pass between Lake Superior and Lake Michigan. The red and green lights, the ships, the sound of moving water, horns, whistles and bells – all of it engaged me in a way that nothing had before. It was almost as if I had been there before, was returning home, or in some way belonged there.

That began a near life-long attraction to anything nautical, and the dream that some day I would be on a ship like those I saw, traveling to distant horizons. After unsuccessful bids for appointments to the U.S. Naval and Coast Guard academies, the dream faded as the course of my studies and work took a different path. Whenever I found myself near a body of water and boats again, though, the pull resumed, and many years later I heeded the call and learned to sail. I seek every opportunity now to become a more proficient sailor, to take longer and more challenging voyages, and to introduce others to sailing.

The pattern in this portion of my "tapestry" is still emerging; for now it takes the shape of using sailing adventures as metaphors for leadership and teamwork. For many years my "call to the sea" was a "loose thread" in my tapestry – a clue for the story that could unfold, but that would remain only a clue until I found that loose thread again and wove it back into my life.

> *The ideal is in thyself; the impediment, too, is in thyself.*
> Thomas Carlyle

I have one more thread in the "Al tapestry" to share, then it will be your turn to "pull on a few of your threads:" A few years ago it dawned on me that my first year of life, as for all of us no doubt, was a significant thread in my life tapestry. In my case, I was born in a hospital where, due to illness, my mom needed to remain for about a year. From several days after birth and for the next year, the majority of my days were spent in foster homes or in the care of my French grandmother who left her home country to help Dad out. Could that have played – and I think it did – a role in my independence, or the frequent "feeling in my bones" that "if it is to be it's up to me"?

On the positive side, this self-reliance and fierce independence have served me well as an independent consultant, a role that at times is accompanied by rejection and periods of insecurity. A "shadow" aspect of this independence is that I can sometimes slip into a sense of "I'm in this all alone." I can think of instances in my life where there were probably many able and willing hands to help me, but because of the shadow aspects of my independent, go-it alone nature, I didn't acknowledge them. So there is a "back side" to our tapestries as well – the side that reveals imperfections that we sometimes want to hide or not acknowledge.

Integrity means acknowledging, accepting and owning all of our story and all of who we are – our strengths as well as our shadows. As Anne Wilson-Schaef, an acclaimed author and resource for healing and healthy living put it: *"You need to claim the events of your life to make yourself yours."*

There are many threads in the tapestries that tell our stories, and each of them holds clues about who we are — virtues, vices, character, aims — the whole story. What are some of the threads in your story?

What are the some threads that provide clues to any pattern in the tapestry of your life?

All stories have "defining moments," or "moments of truth." In an historical novel these are the pivotal events or characters that seem to dictate the course of a life, of a community or of history itself. In a mystery they might be events that provide clues for answering difficult questions or solving a mystery. In the stories that are our lives, these defining moments or moments of truth are also pivotal to the course our lives take, the lessons we learn or values we adopt. What are some "moments of truth" or "defining moments" of your life story so far?

Organizations have "stories" as well. One of my favorite exercises with clients is asking organization members to construct a "history wall," beginning from the organization's origin to the present day. On a continuous roll of paper covering an entire wall, I ask participants to record significant events, milestones and achievements in their organization's history, along with their dates. I ask them to think about times that were positive as well as those that were not, but that in any event were "defining moments" or "moments of truth" – events that say something about what the organization has become, and how. Multiple entries about the same time or event are fine and encouraged, since they reflect the strength and influence of shared memories.

When we all stand back to survey the "history wall" I ask participants to comment on what they see – their or others' entries – and the significance of those times and events. Were they positive or negative experiences, or some of both? Why? What did each significant time or event reflect about the organization's founders, leaders and members? Why do people hold those times and events in their collective memory, and what have they learned from the experiences? What do the events and how people decided and acted at those times suggest about the organization's culture and real values? What long-term impact have these events had on the organization's members and stakeholders?

What are some of your organization's "stories?" What do they reveal about the organization?

What significant times or events were "moments of truth" or "defining moments" for your organization? Why?

How did people's decisions or actions during your organization's "defining moments" say something about the organization's culture — its virtues, real values or perhaps "shadow sides?"

CORE VALUES

Our core values are literally what we value most. To function with integrity it is essential that we be clear about what those values are. We need to exercise some care here and make sure that what we claim to be our values are in fact our values and not ones we think we should have or that are "politically correct." We need to be more conscious about our values so they can be more reliable guides for our decisions and behavior. To do that, it can be useful to replay our past decisions and behavior and be honest about what motives drove them. Whatever did will likely reflect our true values.

If we remain consistently silent about an executive's demeaning or overbearing behavior for example, it may be because we value "security" more than "respect" or "fairness." If we consistently work late and miss our son's or daughter's extra-curricular activities, perhaps we value "achievement" over "family".

> *He who floats with the current, who does not guide himself according to higher principles, who has no ideal, no convictions — such a man is a mere article of the world's furniture — a thing moved, instead of a living and moving being — an echo, not a voice.*
>
> Henri-Frederic Amiel

For values to serve us, guiding decisions and behavior, we need to understand what we really mean by the labels we attach to them. For example consider the varying interpretations of "family" — as in "pro family" or "family values" across political and religious spectrums. To gain more clarity about what our values really mean we can complete a set of "I will" or "I will not" statements. If I say that "financial security" is a value, for example, what would I do and not do to actualize that value? Another useful values clarification exercise is to consider what kinds of decisions or behavior we would consider "heresy," or a major transgression against a value that we profess.

Some find it helpful to lay prospective values out on each axis of a 2 by 2 matrix to make forced-choice comparisons between each value and all the others. Those that consistently rate higher than others suggest which values are primary; those that consistently rate lower than others are likely lower on the importance list or perhaps are not really core values. Such an exercise or thought process can be useful since difficult situations at times require judgment calls between "two rights" or choices among competing values.

As you might guess, "Integrity" is at the top of my list of core values. (And agree or disagree, you will likely know what that means to me by the time you finish this book!) Here is the balance of mine:

Freedom with responsibility
Invest in the next generation
Good work (for me and for others)
Enjoy each day as if it's my last and as if I will account for it another day
Enjoy and respect nature.

What are your core values — what matters most to you? How do you know?

Is there an "order" to your values? Which take precedence over others?

How have your core values driven your decisions and behavior over the years?

Can you remember any times when options for deciding or acting presented "values dilemmas" — when values you have clashed or satisfying one value interfered with satisfying another? Which carried the day?

What times can you remember when acting in alignment with your values required a sacrifice or extracted a price? What did you do and what were the consequences?

ORGANIZATIONS AND THEIR VALUES

Remember the findings from Collins and Porras'[6] research in Chapter One: adherence to core values is a significant contributing factor of sustainable organizational excellence. (Powerful *adaptive mechanisms* were also a factor – a topic that we will take up in Chapter Four on *Alignment*.) Specifically, they found that corporations doggedly adhering to their core values and displaying the ability to adapt over the years consistently yielded returns to stockholders that were on average six times the returns of their comparison companies over a fifty-year period and almost twelve times the return of the overall stock market. Subsequent experience and research indicated a comparable dynamic with private and not-for-profit organizations.

> *Expedients are for the hour, but principles are for the ages. Just because the rains descend and the winds blow, we cannot afford to build on shifting sands.*
> Henry Ward Beecher

Why does adherence to core values have that kind of impact? First, as Alexander Hamilton said: "If we don't know what we stand for, we will fall for anything." And fall they have, recently in greater numbers than usual – be they public officials, organizations or executives. Our values serve as our compass in times of turbulence or uncertainty – pointing the way towards "home," what we set out to accomplish and who we want to be.

At sea there generally are no permanent markings or navigational aids to guide the journey, just like in today's markets and environment there appear to be few or continually shifting landmarks. Leaders and organizations without solid and clearly articulated values are like compasses with no markings; which way is the right way? How do we get our bearings?

Just like personal values, it does little good if organizations don't clearly articulate their values and do all they can to assure understanding of what they mean. "Integrity" is listed as a core value in at least half of the organizations that I encounter, but when I have the opportunity to ask people what that means, there are often spirited discussions and multiple, not always complementary, interpretations. I recently witnessed a vigorous discussion within an executive team about whether "Accountability" was one of their organization's core values. One or two were adamantly opposed to the idea, believing that it reflected more of a "power over" than "empowerment" mentality. You might want to adapt the "will" / "will not" or "values heresy" exercise above with your organization or team to achieve clarity around organizational values and what really matters. When a group sincerely works at articulating its values, by the end of the process all members can be more confident about what they stand for and the level of agreement about values.

> *No enterprise can exist for itself alone. It ministers to some great need, it performs some great service, not for itself, but for others; or failing therein, it ceases to be profitable and ceases to exist.*
> Calvin Coolidge

Like a mission or purpose, values that are primarily self-serving will not have the power to engage workers or attract and retain customers. Values that resonate with those doing the work and with prospective customers are those that motivate the best efforts and customer loyalty. In <u>Be Your Own Brand</u>, David McNally and Karl Speak[7] define a *brand* as a "relationship," and a strong brand as "an accurate reflection of who we really are." In their words, "a branded relationship is a special type of relationship that involves the kind of trust that only happens when parties believe there is a direct connection between their value systems."

Start-up organizations may have an easier time defining their core values; if the founders are clear about what they value and want their organization to stand for, they can articulate those values and design the organization around them. "Designing the organization around them" means hiring people who share those values, rewarding behaviors that reinforce them, disciplining those that do not, providing support and coaching to live out the values and monitoring adherence to the values.

Organizations that have operated for some time without articulated values, those with conflicting values, and those where there is dissonance between stated values and behaviors will have a harder time of it. Leaders in those organizations will need to tap into the "nobler sentiments" of organization members, mining the "values pool" to find the ones that resonate with their customers and that will stir people's best efforts. In organizations where there has been "values abuse," leaders need to break through layers of cynicism as they enter conversations about vision or values.

It's not hard to make decisions when you know what your values are.
Roy Disney

I must admit that when helping leaders and their organizations articulate core values, their lists look very similar. I often see values that are variations of "integrity," "honesty," "service," "excellence," "quality," "trust" and "stewardship." That's fine as long as people truly mean those values; after all, they are the same values and concepts that have motivated people's highest efforts for centuries.

The real value is in what happens before the final list of values is drawn up and also in what happens afterward. What needs to happen before is an organization-wide process of some kind that engages participants, including the organization's leaders, for discerning what their highest values are and need to be. The process here truly is as, or even more, important than the product; it is the conversations like what people care about, what gives them pride, what their customers need, what motivates them and what turns them off that eventually yield understanding about what really matters and what will serve as the organization's compass.

What needs to happen afterward is that the values truly serve as the compass for people's behavior and for the organization. When confronted with choices like investments, potential business directions, hiring, discipline or what to communicate, leaders need to incorporate consideration of values in their deliberations. In my work with many independent physician practices, I witnessed the unraveling of several joint business ventures and merged practices when differences in cultures or practice values were not sufficiently taken into account.

I've watched other physician groups and professional practices struggle and in some cases derail on account of hires that were values mismatches or because of performance standards and pay schemes that sent the wrong messages. Most important, in any organization the leaders, including board members or trustees, need to model the desired values; when they don't, values quickly lose their credibility and their power. The culture and leaders' behavior need to grant "permission" and even encourage feedback or "flags" that call attention to any dissonance between values as stated and values as practiced.

Leaders that do the best job of articulating and modeling their values will be the ones who inspire the greatest trust and engage their followers. Organizations that effectively articulate, model and reinforce values that resonate with their members will win the talent wars in coming years. All who demonstrate values that are important to customers will enjoy distinct competitive advantage.

Does your organization have stated core values or principles? If so, what are they? Are they clear to all?

Whether or not your organization has stated core values or principles, what do you think they are? How do you know?

How compatible are your organization's core values or principles with your own?

Have there ever been situations where you believed you were expected to act in ways that were not aligned with your or your organization's values? What were they, and what did you do? Why?

OUR CHARACTER

The Delphi temple in Greece was home to the Oracle, coun-selor to visitors, travelers and leaders thousands of years ago. In the ruins above its entry, today we can still see the immortal words of Socrates: "Know thyself" – as sound a piece of advice today as it was then. I agree with famed Chicago journalist Sydney Harris who stated "ninety

> *True strength is found not in perfection, but in understanding our own limitations.*
> Annette Simmons

percent of the world's woes come from people not knowing themselves, their abilities, their frailties, and even their real virtues."

Much of what I've witnessed over the years that kept lead-ers from being their best, sometimes derailing their careers and their organizations, stemmed from limited self-awareness. Examples include managers blind to their perfectionism and consequent inability to delegate, doctors with no clue that peers viewed them as belligerent and disrespectful, and skilled profes-sionals who succumbed to "promotions" that took them away from what they were most gifted at doing. Mastering the *Iden-tity* challenge means owning *the whole* of who we are, including our "bright" and "shadow" sides. Organizations have bright and shadow sides as well; knowing both helps them take full advan-tage of their strengths and avoid getting tripped up by limita-tions that they can't see.

> *What you have outside you counts less than what you have inside you.*
> B. C. Forbes

We will likely never be able to fully catalog and mine all facets of our character or personality, but since the last half of the twentieth century psychologists have given us many tools to help. One of many is the popular Myers-Briggs Type Indicator[8], a self-administered survey initially developed by Katherine Briggs and her daughter Isabel Myers over a half-century ago and based largely on Carl Jung's personality research. The MBTI reflects our preference from an early age for *Introversion* (inner life / orientation) vs. *Extraversion* (outer life / orientation), *Sensing* (facts and tangible things) vs. *Intuition* (possibilities and intangible realities), *Thinking* (rational analysis) vs. *Feeling* (sensitivity to feelings, values and less objective factors), and *Perceiving* (openness to new information and slower decision-making) vs. *Judging* (quicker decision-making and closure).

Our pattern across these preferences reflects natural strengths in our approach to the world, problem-solving and decision-making. Knowing these preferences and our strong suits can help us build on them and use them more intentionally. We need to recognize that because they are our preferences and strengths we will favor their use in our approach to the world, problem-solving and decision-making – just like a preference for using our right or left hand.

The opposites of our preferences are of course equally valid, just different. In fact the same differences in preferences or strengths that can lead to misunderstanding and conflict are the very same that can help us solve problems and make decisions more effectively collectively. As measured by the MBTI, I have a preference and natural strength for *Thinking* over *Feeling*, while my wife has the opposite. There are times when I will be ready to act based on purely my "reasoned," more analytical assessment of a situation, but Carley is more in tune with the feelings, values or below-the-surface dimensions of a situation; that was often the case raising our girls.

While these differences in preferences made for some pretty

spirited disagreements and discussions at times, and took longer than if one of us alone had to make a call, they usually resulted in better outcomes – that is if each of us recognized and respected the other's different but equally valid approaches and realities. Of course the fact that both of us have strong preferences for *Intuition* (not very attentive to numbers and specifics) over *Sensing* (very attentive to numbers and details) has led to pretty marginal financial records and gratitude that our financial advisor is gifted differently! Individually and collectively, living up to our promise requires not only acknowledgement of others', but also our own unique strengths.

There are many instruments like the MBTI available to help us better understand our character – our motives, values, preferences, styles and personalities. Since we are complex, with many facets to our character and personality, my bias is to take advantage of as many as possible to help give ourselves a deeper, textured understanding of who we are. (There is a lot of junk out there in the personality / trait profiling business; it is best to acquire them from reputable, licensed sources and to ask about their research base.)

It is hard for most of us to uncover and own our "shadow" sides. Without owning our limitations and vulnerabilities, however, they often control us usually without our awareness – instead of the other way around.

> *I now know myself to be a person of weakness and strength, liability and giftedness, darkness and light. I now know that to be whole means to reject none of it but to embrace all of it.*
>
> Parker Palmer

Unfortunately most of us have probably been in the position of witnessing associates, friends or acquaintances be done-in again and again on account of repetitive behaviors, reactions, habits or characteristics that they somehow just weren't aware of. That's where serial marriages, many repetitive job losses or a string of lost friendships that fail for the same reason come from. Much of Wall Street's and the economy's 2008 breakdown can be attributed to institutions and their leaders that were blind to cultures that rewarded foolhardy risks, repressed disagreement and bad news or cultivated excessive hubris. We can read chilling accounts of them now in books like <u>Nobody Listened</u>[9] (the Madoff scandal), <u>House of Cards</u>[10] (Bear Stearns bankruptcy) and <u>The Devil's Casino</u>[11] (Lehman Brothers' collapse).

How can we reduce our blind sides when we can't see them? That's why they're called "blind spots," right?

Reflecting on our "stories," especially in conjunction with authentic feedback from others, can shed light on potential "shadow" sides of our personality. Some personality measures are also useful. On one such instrument, the Hogan Development Survey, I score fairly high on the *Excitability* dimension – a tendency to over-react or get worked up. While there are times when an emotional reaction may be precisely what's called for and very authentic, there are other times, especially if I'm not aware of my tendency to overreact, when it would likely take away from my credibility and effectiveness. I'm not really sure where the *Excitability* comes from, but knowing that it's part of how I'm put together allows me to do something about it and less likely that it will create a problem.

"360°" surveys that collect anonymous feedback from a leader's followers and peers, especially accompanied by coaching, can also be powerful tools to shed light on blind spots. I remember being asked to coach an insurance executive who had received feedback in a performance review about being impatient and arrogant. He just did not understand how that could be the case and refused to believe it, at least until he saw others' perceptions to that effect in black and white from his 360.

However we acquired them, many of us carry around certain "shadow" beliefs and assumptions. Shadow beliefs and assumptions are ingrained ways of seeing things that are self-limiting or interfere with accurate perception. Some of us for example, based on early experience or messages, may automatically assume that we are not "good enough, strong enough or smart enough" to accomplish a challenge without outside help, or perhaps even that we "don't deserve" to be successful. Rather than seeing a task or challenge for what it is and freely drawing on our skills and resources, such ingrained self-perceptions or internal scripts limit our ability to respond effectively from the beginning.

I value James Thurber's advice: that periodically in our lives it is important to take stock of "what we are running to and what we may be running from." Reflecting on our "stories" can yield clues about what we are running to or from, and how that influences our character. We "run toward" things like early passions in life or activities that employ our natural strengths or advance our purpose, vision and aims – topics explored below. Awareness of those things we

> *All people should strive to learn before they die what they are running from, and to, and why.*
> James Thurber

"run to" helps us understand our natural motivators and ways to leverage our strengths.

Most of us are likely also "running from" something to a greater or lesser extent. Consciously or not, whatever we may be running from can exert strong influence on our behavior; more than likely the effect will be stronger and more negative if we are unaware of the influences. Some may run from a fear of being alone, abandoned or unpopular; some may run from a fear of scarcity; some also may run from a fear of being controlled or manipulated by others. Awareness of what we are "running from" may help us counter irrational fears or better understand filters that interfere with accurately interpreting reality.

Hide not your talents. They for use were made.
Benjamin Franklin

Just as we are sometimes blind to our limitations, we can be equally unaware of our talents and strengths. As Jonathan Swift said: "Although we are accused of not knowing our own weaknesses, yet perhaps few know our own strength. As in soils, sometimes there is a vein of gold which the owner knows not." Reflecting on tasks or times where what to do came naturally for us or when our enjoyment performing the work was matched with equally positive outcomes can inform us about natural or motivated strengths.

Taking advantage of all the ways that we can to become better acquainted with our stories, values, strengths, "shadows" and other dimensions of who we are positions us well for navigating integrity challenges successfully and becoming the best that we can be.

What are five or six adjectives you would use to describe your "character" — distinctive traits, qualities or characteristics that say something about what makes you yourself?

Ask a few of your friends, family members and associates the same question – what are the five or six words or adjectives that come up most often when asked to describe you or what make you yourself?

What would you say your top three or four strengths are? (knowledge, skills, attitudes, aptitudes . . .)

What would you say your top three or four limitations or weaknesses are?

Does it ever seem that you operate with "shadow beliefs" or assumptions (about yourself or others) operating that are self-limiting? ("Scripts" or things you've come to believe from prior experiences, or how you interpreted those experiences, that get in the way of seeing things as they are or effectively responding?)

Since we are not usually very objective when it comes to ourselves, input and feedback from others on all these questions – especially the last one – is a good idea.

ORGANIZATIONS HAVE "CHARACTER" TOO

Organizations, and pockets of organizations, also "grow up" (or don't!) with embedded strengths, limitations, "shadow beliefs" or assumptions, tendencies and characteristics; most call that "culture." Sometimes these are reflections of the founders, owners or leaders; they usually also reflect collective traits and competencies of the organization's members. Going back to the MBTI typologies, for example, an organization with many introverts who prefer facts, details, objectivity and quick decisions – especially if that characterizes leaders' or founders' styles – would have a different culture than one populated with mainly extraverts who have a more intuitive, subjective style – again, especially if that reflected preferences of its founders or leaders. Just as it would be dangerous to characterize individuals based on limited factors or personality dimensions, we need many data points and different kinds of observations to begin sizing up an organization's character or culture.

> *This ability to perceive the limitations of one's own culture and to develop the culture adaptively is the essence and ultimate challenge of leadership.*
> Edgar Schein

Well-designed organizational surveys can help piece together a picture of an organization's culture. Sometimes outside observers of organizations help; just like anthropologists observing tribal or geographical cultures, outsiders can be more adept at understanding an organization's "character." Is the culture entrepreneurial? Fair? Risk-avoidant? Service-driven? Secretive?

Sometimes an organization's character or culture reflects a mindset with origins at critical points or "moments of truth" in the organization's past, reinforced by the retelling of stories about those experiences. One retail client with a strong service orientation, for example, would almost routinely begin or end meetings calling out workers who went to incredible lengths getting an order shipment right or to resolve a customer problem.

On the negative side, a culture characterized by contentious union and management relations might be reinforced by stories of times when there truly was an adversarial relationship between union employees and management. I have worked with some academic and health care institutions where certain longer-tenured and influential members of the teaching or medical side of the community almost ritually retold the "sins" of administration from earlier years – and of course administrators would tell the same kind of stories about the other side. (I am often surprised that some such stories go back ten to twenty years and no longer reflect current reality; we will touch on that dynamic in the next chapter.) True or not, stories and mindsets like these reflect important facets of an organization's culture.

It is especially important on long crossings or when there are possibilities of rough seas to have detailed knowledge of a boat's characteristics, capabilities, "quirks" and limitations. Likewise, it will be important for leaders to not only know themselves well, but also their organizations' characteristics, capabilities and quirks for the surely challenging conditions ahead.

What are some one or two-word descriptors you would use to reflect your organization's culture?

What aspects of your organization's culture would you say will serve you well in coming years?

What aspects of your organization's culture might interfere with its ability to live up to its promise in the years ahead??

As with self-awareness, sometimes our own assessment of our organization's culture may not be as accurate as we think. What methods might you use to gain a more accurate picture of your organization's culture, its bright spots and potential vulnerabilities?

WHAT IS YOUR BUSINESS?

Translate "business" here as "mission," or as the French say: "raison d'etre" (reason for being.) At the individual level, our "business" is our sense of purpose, or calling. It is for some people what it seems they were made for, of what James Hillman, in <u>The Soul's Code</u>, refers to as the seeds of our character, or "the plot of our story." When we are fully engaged with our purpose or calling, we have what William James refers to as that "particular mental or moral attitude in which, when it comes upon us, we feel ourselves deeply and intensively active and alive. At such moments there is a voice inside which speaks and says, "This is the real me."

> *Purpose is the most essential core of leadership. Without purpose there is no mission, vision or reason for being.*
> Tom Votel

In his first edition of <u>The Power Of Purpose</u>, Richard Leider[12] cites research that he conducted by interviewing a cross-section of adults over 65. In answer to the question: "If you could live your life over again, what would you do differently?" The older adults consistently responded that they would be more reflective, more courageous, and clearer about their purpose earlier. In a workshop I conducted for a group of nursing home administrators, one of them made this observation: "I've often thought, Al, that those in our homes who seem the saddest are those who regret that they haven't lived their lives with more integrity."

My guess is that part of what she saw were people late in life who hadn't lived their lives "on purpose" as Leider would say – who were afraid they had not lived up to their promise and would "die with their music still inside of them." Navigating the *Identity* challenge successfully requires an ear for whatever may be calling us to serve. A sense of purpose that has meaning is foundational for living up to our promise and potential.

Have you ever seen a *"Born to _____ (run / win / sail/ take your pick)"* tattoo? I often thought how convenient it would be if we came into this world "tattooed" in such a manner. But as our younger daughter Kristin pointed out to me a number of years ago: "Yeah, Papa, but then we wouldn't have the fun of discovering what that is!" – wise beyond her years, I guess.

Perhaps it's easier for some than for others to discern their true purpose given strong interests, early evidence of unique talents, heritage or circumstances. For most of us it is a discovery or discernment process, requiring attunement to those times when our values, interests and talents intersect with others' needs or work that needs doing.

I prefer short mission or purpose statements; they force very intentional phrasing and therefore thought, and are easy to remember and therefore more likely to keep us focused. If not a tattoo, think of what you might print on your own personal "bumper sticker." To help you draft that:

What are your "motivated strengths" — tasks you are drawn to or are particularly good at?

Toward what end? When you exercise those motivated strengths or perform those tasks, why do you want to, and for whom? What do you hope the results will be and what do you hope will be accomplished?

Now try stringing your thoughts together into a coherent ten- or twelve-word statement that captures the essence of work you think you are meant to do, that provides meaning for you and makes a contribution of some kind.

Are you living your purpose now? If so, how? If not, why not? What changes that you can initiate would likely lead to living and working in closer alignment with your purpose?

These days it's hard to find an organization without a stated mission or purpose statement. We can be sure that even Washington Mutual, Wachovia, Lehman Brothers and other "washouts" from disasters that unfolded in 2008 all had printed mission statements. Harder to find are organizations where there is real shared ownership for the mission and a sense that efforts, systems and processes are strongly aligned with that mission.

Whether organizational or personal, an authentic mission serves to ground us and maintain focus, as do clearly articulated values. When there is turmoil or confusion, or when everything seems to be shifting under our feet, it is helpful to remember why we are there. To paraphrase the old axiom: "When we're up to our you-know-whats in alligators, it's helpful to remember that our purpose is to drain the swamp!"

> *If things are not going well with you, begin your effort at correcting the situation by carefully examining the service you are rendering, and especially the spirit in which you are rendering it.*
> Roger Babson

On a personal level, for example, when I experience performance anxiety over a big presentation, I find it very calming and focusing to simply remember what my purpose is – not about me, and to remember who I am doing it for. Likewise, when facilitating a particularly difficult conversation it's helpful for me to remember what the big-picture intent of the discussion is and to remind participants of what we are trying to accomplish.

> *Purpose is the difference between good and great, between honorable success and legendary performance, between fifteen minutes of fame and a legacy.*
> Nikos Mourkogiannis

For organizations, clarity and agreement around purpose, as with values, serves as a kind of "self-guiding" mechanism. For example a clear purpose can serve as an important filter for which opportunities to pursue and which to dismiss. "Custom manufacturing" was an important element in one client's mission statement. A major component of their competitive edge was their core competency for manufacturing low-tolerance, extremely precise parts to custom specifications. Being clear about their purpose and commitment to "custom manufacturing" helped them pass on an acquisition. The deal looked attractive initially, but the company for sale wasn't a fit with my client's custom manufacturing focus; its acquisition would have sent mixed messages to their market and diluted their competitiveness.

> When any organization is defined by an arbitrary division between the so-called facts of institutional life and the institution's values, the institution's basic identity is eroded.
>
> Thomas Holland and David Hest

An organization's mission statement is its primary "promise" to those it serves; health organizations promise to heal, academic institutions promise to educate, governing bodies promise to govern for the public good, etc. mission integrity erodes, brands are devalued and organizations fail to live up to their promise when it becomes about something else. "No margin, no mission" is a reality for not-for-profit hospitals and academic institutions, for example, but when margin becomes the mission, they fail the *Identity* challenge. Governing bodies are typically composed of elected representatives, but when it becomes about solely getting votes or making another party look bad instead of public service, they too fall short.

Mission integrity is also compromised if we confuse "scorecards" with our core purpose – even if the scorecards are "balanced." "Number of students enrolled" or "number of patients served," for example, really does not tell us much about how an academic institution is actually delivering on its promise to improve learning or how a health clinic is living up to its promise of improving community health.

Publicly held corporations experience constant pressure to deliver on financial expectations to the point where delivering on their true purpose can become compromised. Of course all, particularly investor-owned, organizations need to pay attention to financial performance. If that were their primary purpose, however, all organizations would have the same mission – to make as much money as possible, and having the same mission as any other organization is not the foundation for an enduring organization that contributes value.

To stay on mission in rapidly changing environments and markets requires innovation, but that innovation must be consistent with the organization's core purpose; otherwise "mission integrity" suffers. Starbucks' initial efforts to expand offerings beyond excellent coffee to include retail music and later quick breakfasts might have been innovative, but threatened its mission integrity and devalued the brand. 2008 Wall Street and bank failures were driven in large part by financial products and investment vehicles that were so "innovative," few even understood them, let alone could say with confidence that they were consistent with their issuers' missions and values.

We should not confuse staying on mission with sticking only to ways that we've achieved our purpose in the past. Organizations become less and less relevant over time by clinging too long to ways that worked for achieving those outcomes historically instead of adopting approaches that could lead to superior outcomes. Polaroid would not have lost its position as an industry leader if in the '80s and '90s it was more open to exploring digital imaging for photos instead of focusing research on what it had always been good at – instant film. Getting better and better at the videotape distribution business was a hopeless cause as DVDs, cable and satellite channels ramped up.

What is your organization's purpose or mission? (It is probably written somewhere, but if not or even before looking, try crafting one from your understanding — along the lines of your personal mission format from earlier: <u>what</u> your organization does, <u>why</u> or for what reason, <u>for whom</u> and anything unique about how the organization does what it does.)

Would you say that your organization is "on purpose" — delivering on its main promise to customers and demonstrating high mission integrity?

Do you sense any mission erosion or threats to your organization's mission integrity — like confusing "margin" and "mission," being distracted by "scorecards" or stubbornness around traditional ways?

How aligned do you feel your personal purpose is with your organization's purpose? Do you think that fulfilling your purpose is helping your organization achieve its purpose — and vice-versa?

WHERE ARE YOU GOING?

As the Cheshire Cat told Alice in Wonderland: "If you don't know where you want to go, then any road will take you there." Navigating the *Identity* challenge is not about taking "any road," though, but a road that is consistent with our purpose, values and aims. Character, culture, purpose and values form the foundation of our identity, or *promise*. Our aims – what we intend to do, be or accomplish – in a sense our *"promises,"* are our commitments to act in ways that are consistent with who we are – *identity* in the "future perfect tense," if you will. Here we switch from *identity* as who we are to *identity* as who we want to be or what we hope to accomplish.

> Undoubtedly, we become what we envisage.
>
> Claude M. Bristol

I don't want to get tangled in the jumble of terms that have evolved for different types or levels of aims, intentions and plans, but I do think there is a hierarchy of some kind that is helpful for personal and organizational goal setting. At the highest level is what most would call a "vision," which I think of as literally a "picture" in our mind's eye of an ideal or highly desirable future that we hope to attain. A vision might be several paragraphs or condensed to a few short statements or perhaps just a few words.

The process of *envisioning* is usually as, or maybe is more important, than the product because it prompts us to connect with images of what we hope to attain and of what motivates us or pulls us in the right direction. In an organization or community, there can be great value envisioning an ideal future together as participants discover common ground and explore differences. While a vision should be a stretch to fire our imaginations and motivate effort, it should reflect a future that is attainable, not a fantasy.

Not much is required to begin capturing a vision except the opportunity to be reflective, exercise our imaginations and capture the images that come to mind. I usually facilitate the process for clients using a guided-imagery exercise where I ask them to envision things like what incredible success looks like in a few years, what others are saying about them and the organization, what barriers they have overcome and how, what they are celebrating and any other graphic images that come to mind as they picture a great future.

This is an exercise that works for individuals as well as for organizations or groups. At some point, of course, it's helpful to examine the degree to which our personal visions are complementary with our organization's or our community's. Is the future we envision for ourselves and our loved ones compatible with the vision and aims of where we work or where we live? It may not be possible, for example, to realize our vision of a contemplative, reflective life with time to finish a novel and travel with friends if we are signed up to help a start-up entrepreneurial technology firm reach its vision to grow and go public.

What do you envision / dream for yourself? Take a few moments and record some notes – mentally or otherwise – of your ideal future in ten years . . . five years . . . (You pick the time frame, but a vision is your longer-term horizon, so at least three years from now.) Don't edit; capture whatever images come to mind in as much detail as you can.

Don't feel constrained by these questions, but use them as "prompts" for your vision if they are helpful:

Where are you in your vision? Where are you living?

How are you spending your time? If you are working, what are you doing? . .

Who are you doing it with and for?

What do you like about what you are doing?

What are you doing outside of work that gives you satisfaction? Why is that rewarding?

Who are you spending time with? What is enjoyable about that?

What are you celebrating as you envision your ideal future? What goals have you achieved . . . what have you accomplished that you always hoped for . . . what obstacles have you overcome?

Capture whatever additional images and details come to mind as you envision your ideal future.

Remember, a vision is a "realistic dream" — a stretch, but attainable for you.

If your organization has a "vision," what is it?

Do you see yourself in your organization's vision? How congruent is it with your own?

What might you do as a leader of your organization or group to sharpen its vision and make it more compelling?

"Strategies," "goals" and "objectives," or some variations of those, are usually next in the hierarchy of mechanisms for capturing our aims — what or where we hope to be. I like comparing a "vision" to the horizon — an attractive destination that beckons. In that vein, strategies are basic decisions we make or directions we take to achieve a vision and reach our horizon.

If a man does not know what port he is steering for, no wind is favorable to him.

Seneca

Two alternative business strategies, for example, are to basically follow a "cost leadership" or "differentiation" strategy — both of which can be a successful route to growth and profitability. Southwest and Virgin Atlantic have both been relatively successful, profitable airlines. Southwest Airlines pursues more of a cost leadership strategy with few traveler amenities, no reserved seating (for many years, at least) and a focus on being the lowest-cost choice serving relatively limited markets. Virgin Atlantic offers an array of traveler amenities, multiple classes and price levels of reserved seating and more traveler legroom, and has consistently made significant investments in marketing information infrastructure.

On a personal level, some may pursue the strategy of a higher education, and perhaps prestigious advanced degrees on their road to

The most important thing about having goals is having one.
Geoffrey F. Abert

"life, liberty and the pursuit of happiness." A more suitable path for others, however, may be to eschew advanced degrees or a highly specialized professional education in favor of the trades, the military or a less intense work regimen that allows time for more avocations. All such strategies are viable options; fortunately we are free to choose (at least in some countries) which paths to follow. To meet the identity challenge and live up to our promise it is important that we choose which path is best suited for our combination of vision, values, interests, capabilities and character. That requires that we know ourselves well – and if it is not a conventional choice or one that provides the most security or financial rewards – that we exercise the courage to make the choice that we believe is the best fit anyway.

To use another nautical analogy, our vision is the horizon and our strategy might be choosing to head for our destination by power or by sail. (We could choose to go by "motor-sailor," but as with cost-leadership or differentiation business strategies, trying to be both usually means not doing either very well!) Think about "goals" and "objectives" then as "waypoints," intermediate destinations, or necessary tasks while we are underway.

We need to have "smart" objectives (Specific, Measurable, Achievable, Relevant and Time-bound) just as we need to be precise about waypoints. We can head off happily into the sunrise, but if we are unsure or unclear about intermediate destinations or tasks we will end someplace other than where we hoped to be (perhaps on the rocks!) Those intermediate destinations and tasks are the *promises* we must keep so we can achieve our vision – the horizon.

Reflect on your personal vision from page 57. What are some basic strategies, or big-picture ways that are alternative paths you might follow to achieve your vision?

Can you settle on a few, or perhaps one approach or strategy that seems best suited for you and what you hope to accomplish? Make some notes of what that would look like. (This is a question that could take an evening of quiet reflection or much longer, perhaps coupled with input and feedback from friends.)

Given your vision – or "horizon" of an ideal future – and the basic strategies or approach you have in mind, what are some of your key "waypoints" or goals and objectives (intermediate destinations or tasks to accomplish)? Be specific enough here so at some point you will be able to tell if you have achieved an objective or "kept your promise."

What are some ways you might help more clearly articulate your organization's or group's vision, strategies, goals and objectives?

IDENTITY – KEY POINTS

Our *Identity* is integrity's foundation; before we can be and stand up for who we are, we need to know who we are. To reach their whole potential, leaders and organizations alike need to be clear about their purpose, values, aims and unique character or culture. We need to understand these fundamentals about our identity: First, we are individuals and social beings; likewise, organizations are independent as well as social entities; neither organizations nor leaders will live up to their full promise without fully inhabiting both identities. Second, we are not only "humans doing," but "humans being;" living up to our full promise involves more than fulfilling whatever work, professional or functional roles we occupy. Third, we need to inhabit all dimensions of who we are – physical, mental, emotional and spiritual.

Our *stories* – "moments of truth" and patterns in the "tapestries" of our lives and organizations can shed light on our character or culture, values, motivations and sense of purpose. The better we understand our personal character and our organization's cultures – the bright and shadow sides, the more likely we can leverage our strengths and limit damage due to blind spots.

Mastering the *Identity* challenge requires a clear declaration of our core values and purpose – those dimensions of our identity that serve to ground us while we adapt, which we must to accomplish our goals.

We are also our intentions, or aims – our identities in the "future perfect" tense. Our intentions and aims are those declarations or promises that we make to ourselves and to others about where we will go, what we aspire to achieve and how we will serve. At the highest level, leaders and organizations can craft visions – graphic pictures of aspirations and goals. To engage others and organize efforts for achieving our vision and stated purpose requires committing to concrete strategies, goals and objectives.

> For years, copying other people,
> I tried to know myself.
> From within, I couldn't decide what to do.
> Unable to see, I heard my name being called.
> Then I walked outside.
> Rumi

CHAPTER 3 | *AUTHENTICITY*

Sometimes, leadership differs from non-leadership only in that leadership views the world with a slightly larger lens.
John Carver

Go put your creed into your deed.
Ralph Waldo Emerson

The truth is more important than the facts.
Frank Lloyd Wright

If any man seeks for greatness, let him forget greatness and ask for truth, and he will find both.
Horace Mann

There is a lot of talk about "authenticity" these days. We seek authentic relationships, authentic experiences, authentic products, authentic cooking and authentic stories. Meeting our economic, social and political challenges will require authentic institutions and leaders. Those leaders and those organizations will be ones that master *Trueness*, *Truth* and *Transparency*.

You've got to be original, because if you are like somebody else, what do they need you for?
Bernadette Peters

TRUENESS

Two rabbis were talking one day about a third rabbi, Rabbi Kaufmann, whom they both admired. One of them, Rabbi Schwartz, confided to his friend that he hoped God wasn't displeased that he wasn't more like Rabbi Kaufmann. And his friend responded: "Are you ever concerned that perhaps God wishes at times that you were more like Rabbi Schwartz?" I remind myself of that story occasionally to help me resist the temptation of wishing I could be more like, or as accomplished as, so- and-so. As William Channing, the early nineteenth-century prominent preacher said: "Every human being is intended to have a character of his own; to be what no other one is, and to do what no other can do." The Wizard from the 1960s cartoon show *Rocky and Bullwinkle* put it even more plainly: "Be what you is, not what you is not!" Authenticity means trueness to our purpose, values and aims, or to paraphrase the caddy in *The Legend of Baggar Vance*, "To play the game that only we were meant to play."

> *Becoming a leader is synonymous with becoming yourself. It is precisely that simple, and it is also that difficult.*
>
> Warren Bennis

Meeting the *Identity* challenge – including clarity about mission, values and aims – lays the foundation for *Authenticity*; leaders and organizations meet the *Trueness* challenge when they are true to those missions, values and aims. They do not claim to be one thing or have one purpose when in fact their energy is devoted to being something else or accomplishing other aims.

A while back I heard an observation that I'm afraid might be true: that "80% of our troubles are on account of people trying to make things appear other than what they really are." To that I would add: "or becoming something other than what one set out to be." Not long ago a business periodical raised the question of whether top-flight business schools, in the interest of boosting their placement ratings ("confusing the scorecard with the game,") are gravitating from their original purpose of educating critical and well-rounded business thinkers by focusing too narrowly on skills demanded by corporate recruiters and investment bankers – essentially becoming glorified trade schools. Some churches have been criticized in recent years for shifting emphasis from their spiritual foundations and true mission to more "market friendly" strategies so they can increase membership and improve their finances.

Upon the *Wall Street Journal's* acquisition by Rupert Murdoch, the journalistic community and the *Journal's* staff expressed serious fears about erosion of journalistic integrity in the interest of luring advertisers and achieving investors' goals. Not long ago Howard Schultz, founder of Starbucks Corporation, raised questions about whether Starbucks' drive for growth and efficiency was diluting "the Starbucks experience" and leading to commoditization of its brand. To me Mr. Schultz was modeling authentic leadership by asking the critical question: "Are we being true to our promise? Are we fulfilling our mission?"

> The shortest and surest way to live with honor in this world is to be in reality what we would appear to be.
> Socrates

I was saddened by the decline of Krispy Kreme doughnuts a few years back. I remember my first near-Nirvana introduction to a Krispy Kreme doughnut fresh off the line in a humble NYC bakery about a dozen years ago; I was hooked. Since Minneapolis was not yet blessed with its own Krispy Kreme outlet, I would make a point on business trips out of town to bring a box of fresh Krispy Kremes back for friends and clients.

Krispy Kreme caught on nationally, and when it went public and began expanding rapidly, its stock caught fire. I thought I had missed a great investment opportunity until a couple years later when I saw my first box of Krispy Kremes on the end-rack of a local big-box retailer. They were of course not the same Krispy Kremes that I experienced in New York or that millions had waited patiently in line for as they came fresh and gooey out of the oven. Krispy Kreme was not living up to its promise, and of course before long, neither was its stock.

I find it useful to remember that early in this country corporate charters were considered a privilege and very few were granted. The original intent of granting corporate charters was to allow pooling of capital and resources in order to accomplish work for the public good like building bridges, canals or dams; enabling shareholders to profit was a means to those ends. I wonder how many business ventures granted incorporation rights today would be considered true to the original intent for corporations to serve the public good? How far have we strayed from the original purpose of corporations to be instruments for advancing common welfare to "anything goes?" (I was going to add "as long as it is not illegal or immoral," but I fear we have long passed that point.)

Most of us have probably been in situations where someone's or an organization's "actions were so loud that we could not hear what they were saying," to paraphrase Emerson. Probably the number one, and most public, indicator of authentic leadership and authentic organizations is that they "walk their talk" and that their "deeds match their creeds." Conversely, leaders and organizations that are not living their values or the principles they espouse are among the greatest contributors to staff cynicism, disengagement and customer disaffection.

A classic example of organizational authenticity and

integrity is Johnson & Johnson, which in 1982 – at an estimated cost of $100 million – removed all of its Tylenol products anywhere they were sold after seven people in the Chicago area died taking Tylenol tablets. (It was learned later that a non-J&J employee had tampered with the tablets and laced them with cyanide.) At great additional cost, the company launched a 2,500-person effort to notify the public of the problem - again not because it had to, but because a J&J core value was to put customers and their safety first. Further, J&J led the way developing the tamper-proof medicine containers that we have today.

Contrast that with the spate of recent banks and investment firms that failed, most of which claimed to have some variation of a mission to protect assets or grow wealth. As it turns out most of the failed institutions' promises were backed up primarily with shaky mortgage-backed derivatives, questionable investment products that their issuers didn't fully understand, and a few Ponzi schemes thrown in. Not too long before our latest crisis, insurance companies that promised variations of improving financial security or making dreams come true were found guilty of luring elderly clients into the purchase of annuities that actually reduced financial security and produced dreams that were only nightmares.

> *The essence of an organization lies in what it believes, what it stands for, and what it values. An organization's works, rather than its words, are the telling assessment of its beliefs.*
>
> John Carver

Of course one line of reasoning or weak defense for offering questionable products or services is "But it's common practice; everyone is doing it!" or "It's just business; if we don't our competitors will." Integrity, however, requires walking our talk and standing by our principles – even when that comes at a cost. Many heroes in our story and history books who stood up for their principles paid with their lives, as many do today who are committed to freedom. The cost for the rest of us is far less, but the dividends are high – in self-respect, confidence, others' empowerment and the trust we earn.

Competitive and market pressures, a drive for growth, investor expectations or distractions veiled as opportunities make it difficult to stay "on mission" unless we are very clear about our purpose and values. Most hospitals state some variation of a mission to provide high quality medical treatment and to improve the health of their communities; most hospitals are also organized as not-for-profit organizations.

To survive, let alone thrive as a corporation, any hospital needs to pay very close attention to costs, productivity improvement and healthy financial performance – after all, "no margin, no mission." Some however, including a few states' attorney generals, have questioned whether certain not-for-profit hospitals are truly "not-for-profit" given their operations and financial models. One common standard for a hospital to be granted non-profit designation is significant use of operating margin for community benefit. I read not long ago about one Chicago hospital's designation as a non-profit being challenged by its state attorney general for counting salaries to its employees as part of what it was giving back to the community. When salaries weren't counted, the hospital didn't come near the required community benefit hurdle rate to qualify as a true non-profit. (This organization and others like it would no doubt have difficulty passing not only the *trueness* test, but also a *truthfulness* test. It seemed to be engaging in the practice of *"strategic misrepresentation,"* the actual name for an executive education seminar that I saw promoted by a prestigious university early in my career.)

The *trueness* issue here is whether market, competitive and financial pressures caused the hospitals to migrate from "no margin, no mission" to "margin <u>as</u> mission." Some academic institutions succumb to similar "identity crises" when pressure for ranking, recruitment costs or efforts to attract high-profile athletic programs lead to margin supplanting mission. A prominent upstate New York university was recently in the news on account of a report documenting how it compromised its academic standards in order to build a winning men's basketball program.

Trueness – faithfulness to our purpose and values – can be at risk at the personal and professional level when contemplating job changes that come veiled as opportunities. Gifted doctors who accept roles with significant management responsibility, or talented professors and researchers who "move up" to administrative roles in their institutions can discover this. I have always admired professionals and workers with the integrity to know who they are and who they are not and with the courage to be true to who they are.

> *Follow the grain in your own wood.*
> Howard Thurman

About twenty years ago, a friend landed an engineering job with a technology company that was a great fit for his technical and mechanical orientation and talents. I always knew him as a gifted "tinkerer" with a knack for figuring out all things mechanical and electronic; he also had a history of little patience for the politics or administrative aspects of organizational life, and for that reason was never interested in any supervisory or managerial work.

Sure enough his employer soon offered him a supervisory assignment – perhaps mistakenly considering that to be a reward for his technical contributions or misjudging his true motivations and talents. When he declined, the pressure only increased; despite the overtures and significantly higher pay potential, he managed to "stay true to his colors" for a number of years. I am convinced that both my friend and his organization would have better lived up to their promise if things remained that way.

Make your work to be in keeping with your purpose.

Leonard Da Vinci

Unfortunately they did not; organizations being what they are, his options for continuing to follow a technical path diminished, and my friend eventually acquiesced to supervisory, then eventually managerial roles. Two years ago, at age fifty-eight, his doctor strongly advised him to quit his job and the organization; the doctor's opinion was that if he didn't, he would likely not live another year. I'm glad that he followed his doctor's advice; when we meet now he is a much happier, healthier man – and back to tinkering and figuring out anything mechanical or electronic.

I met with an associate recently who announced that after thirty years of practicing law, she decided to give up her license. After a period of personal and professional "soul searching" she came to the conclusion that while membership in the bar had allowed her to achieve certain goals – mainly financial – it had been feeling more like a "marriage of convenience" for a number of years.

Her gifts and passions were inclined otherwise, and while she was not certain yet what form they would take, she recognized what was <u>not</u> her. Exercising the discernment to have that realization and act on it freed her up so she could find and follow paths that were better fits for who she was and that would help her live up to her promise.

Remaining true to purpose and principles in the face of competitive and market pressures requires *moral imagination* – creative thinking and the ability to generate new strategies and solutions to meet seemingly incompatible demands. It was moral imagination that stimulated the discovery of materials and methods for carpet manufacturing that were environmentally friendly and competitive. It was moral imagination that led to investment funds

> *If we have no faith in the principles with which we build life, we are defeated.*
> W.N. Thomas, D.D.

like Calvert or Domini Social Investments that yield competitive (and in some cases superior) returns with portfolios that meet social responsibility criteria. I suspect that this moral imagination correlates strongly with highly prized creative thinking in general and with factors that engage a workforce and build customer loyalty.

Authenticity requires *trueness* to our aims as well; we need to keep the end in mind. Sometimes it is easy to get distracted by performance anxiety, a need to look good or other ego matters. In those situations the best antidote for me is to remind myself about why I am there and what my or a group's goals are. When facilitating some of those challenging client meetings, when participants disagree and are at loggerheads, it is helpful to refocus them on their original purpose and goals – for the meeting, for their organization and for their relationships.

Many "integration" efforts that stem from mergers or acquisitions fail the *trueness* test. They get derailed by an inability to remain focused on the vision for combining in the first place, or on the benefits sought for customers and investors. Instead, and usually not openly, efforts are directed to maintaining the status quo or security, increasing power and influence, or other ego-driven intentions. Integrity requires remembering who we are and remaining focused on why we are there and what it was we set out to accomplish. As Benjamin Disraeli observed: "The secret of success is constancy to purpose."

Trueness means keeping our promises and commitments, including any promises we make just to ourselves – like a goal of starting our own company, writing a book, exercising more or reconnecting with friends. A physician client once shared one of the most impressive personal practices I encountered for staying true to our promises. No matter how busy, he always took a few moments near the end of his day to reflect on any commitments he had made to anyone, if he was keeping them and what he needed to do to honor them. Of course committing to take time each day for that reflection was in itself a "promise;" exercising the discipline to honor that commitment helped him be true to other promises he made.

> Never promise
> more than you
> can perform.
> Publilius Syrus

Typically around the beginning of a year, organizations make promises that take the form of goals and objectives – perhaps to grow market share, increase productivity or margins, improve morale or reduce waste. *Trueness* means coming through on those commitments as well. If it appears that we may not achieve announced goals, authenticity requires honesty with ourselves and with others about why. Perhaps knowing what we know now they were and are the wrong goals to pursue; better to know that sooner than later before going faster and faster in the wrong direction.

Perhaps inability to achieve goals that we set is a function of not having seen things clearly or realistically. I am a believer in "stretch" goals; they challenge the status quo as well as our imaginations and have the capacity to motivate excellence. However, too much stretch is debilitating instead of motivating, and I fear that more and more organizations are being pushed to or elect to set impossible goals given their resources or capabilities.

I encounter true burnout in organizations like these – a sense of resignation around what people perceive as unreasonable demands. Instead of rising to meet the challenge of inspirational goals, people feel overwhelmed by expectations that leave them literally out of breath. Performance and sustainability suffer, hopes for any kind of life / work balance are dashed and the credibility of senior leaders erodes. Meeting the *Authenticity* challenge requires the ability to see the nature of tasks to be performed, deadlines and resource constraints realistically.

Think back to your "vision" and big goals from Chapter Two. In what ways would you say you are being true to your vision and goals? What are some examples of being on course?

Again thinking about your vision and big goals, what are some ways or things you could do to be even truer to your aims?

Review your personal values and principles from Chapter Two. What are examples of how you have been or are being true to those values and principles?

What are some ways or things you can do to bring your actions more in line with your personal values and principles?

To what degree do you think your work is in tune with who you are — your interests, gifts and talents, versus burdening you to be who you are not? What changes might bring your work more in line with who you are?

Take a few moments to think of any commitments or promises you made to anyone recently. How have you done keeping those commitments? Is there anything you intend doing to follow up on any of them?

Think of an organization you are part of. What "grade" would you give it in terms of fulfilling its mission or stated purpose? What are examples of ways it does that and perhaps ways that it does not?

What grade would you give that same organization for how it lives up to its stated values and principles? What are examples of ways it does that and perhaps ways it does not?

What are some other aims (ends, commitments, goals or objectives) the organization has made, and how is the organization doing keeping those commitments?

TRUTH

An interesting magazine about science and scientists crossed my desk a while back[1]. The issue's theme was "Truth" and it profiled scientists for whom, as Einstein put it, "the pursuit of truth is more important than its possession." Authentic leaders and organizations, like those scientists, are also "truth-seekers." They acknowledge that they will never possess <u>the truth</u>, but only approximations of truth. That reality does not prevent them from seeking it out anyway; that way at least their approximations get closer and closer to seeing things for what they are.

Self-awareness – learning those things that are true about ourselves – is our first challenge. In the words of Edward White Benson, nineteenth-century author: "How desperately difficult it is to be honest with oneself. It is much easier to be honest with other people." Part of why we rarely know "the truth" is because our histories, unique traits, points of view and limitations inevitably result in at least partial distortions. I'm not sure where I first heard it, but it's true that "with any communication or understanding there is at least some miscommunication or misunderstanding."

> *In the long run, digging for truth has always proved not only more interesting but more profitable than digging for gold.*
>
> George R. Harrison

I do not see your actual behavior or hear what you are really saying; instead I interpret what you say and do through filters and likely distortions that are products of my story, personality characteristics and state of mind. Unless I am aware of those filters and distortions, I will make decisions and act (and likely react) based on a false understanding of what's really going on. Then, you might respond by reacting through your own set of filters and distortions. It's a wonder if we ever reach an understanding or find common ground.

The clearer our "inside view," the better our "outside view;" greater self-awareness arms us with a better understanding of how our personal filters impact our interpretations of reality. In his book <u>A Hidden Wholeness</u>, Parker Palmer[2] re-tells the Taoist tale by Chuang Tzu of *The Woodcarver*, Khing. It was only after Khing withdrew from the world, fasted, detached himself from any worldly fears or thoughts of gain and meditated that he was able to create an exceptional woodcarving because he could "see the right tree and the carving in the tree." One of Parker's takes from the tale is

> *Every man has three characters — that which he exhibits, that which he has, and that which he thinks he has.*
> Alphonse Karr

that "When we do not see ourselves clearly, we can see the other only through 'a glass darkly.'" But when we are clear about our own identities, as the woodcarver was about his, we can be clear about the identity of others as well as how we should act.

As I write this I am reflecting on individuals I've known in leadership positions that lost their place (literally) on account of inability, or perhaps refusal, to see and acknowledge what was really going on. In some cases it had to do with the inability to see or acknowledge serious threats to the financial or competitive positions of their organizations. More commonly, it had to do with inability to see or acknowledge their own limitations around communication, learning from mistakes, making tough calls or their impact on others.

When we are blind to how our own lenses, filters, points of view or traits distort the meaning of what we hear, see or experience we are doubly blind: Not only are we blind to reality or mistakenly in belief that we posses the truth, but we are blind to how we are blind and are bound to suffer the consequences again and again without improving our vision.

Leadership and authenticity – being in touch with reality or the truth of an experience, require presence; we can only be authentic when we are fully present in the here and now. Today, right now, is the only reality; yesterday is history and tomorrow doesn't exist. Far too often we respond or react to right now's experience when we are elsewhere. We make a sales call or attend today's meeting still smarting from yesterday's rejection, so we are half-present with yesterday's self-limiting mindset. We may want to hear about our spouse's or child's day, but instead of being fully present we are thinking about the big meeting tomorrow that we need to prepare for. Instead of really

> *The truth is not simply what you think it is; it is also the circumstances in which it is said, and to whom, why and how it is said.*
>
> Vaclav Havel

listening to fully understand what someone is saying right now, we project what we think he or she means or will say or we plan what we will say next. All of us are victims of our own prejudices or pre-judgments. Instead of experiencing a person as she or he really is, we experience someone that he or she reminds us of. "We do not see things as they are, we see them as we are," as Anais Nin, the famed French diarist, put it.

Not long ago I had one of those very trying experiences with my phone company's "Customer Support" (At times I'm still not sure why they call it that!) automated menus, then an even more trying experience with a testy support rep. When it became apparent that we just "weren't communicating" she handed me up the chain; it was all I could do to just start over in an even tone as a new experience instead of contami-

Most of the basic truths of life sound absurd at first hearing.
Elizabeth Goudge

nating that conversation with carry-over resentment from my last one. I'm glad that I could manage that, since that person was actually very helpful; I'm sure the outcome would not have been as positive had I contaminated the conversation with what preceded it.

Of course if we didn't base our judgments and decisions on prior experience and observations to some degree we might get little accomplished and quickly become dysfunctional. If we seek more authenticity and clearer vision, however, we could all benefit from using more of today's eyes and ears, and less of yesterday's; as Marcel Proust said, "Sometimes the real voyage of discovery begins not so much by seeking new lands but seeing with new eyes."

Authenticity requires being fully present and awake to reality. Feedback can help. If we have the courage to solicit and attend to honest opinions, and actually open ourselves up to the possibility that how we see things may not be exactly how it is, it's amazing how much clearer things get. Sometimes feedback just doesn't get through, however; I have coached some who even when confronted with pretty frank, consistent and negative "360°" feedback couldn't wake up to reality.

I know that I've been blind at times to the reality of what was going on or to my situation when a better understanding of what was blocking my view would have paid many dividends. Things "just not going our way" again and again or finding ourselves in the same predicaments consistently are usually signs that we are blind to some truths about ourselves. For example, if interactions with someone consistently end in disagreements or misunderstanding, it may be time to examine how we are contributing to that. If we seem to consistently be the last to hear news or are always uninformed, it's probably time to examine how we play a role.

If you do not tell the truth about yourself, you cannot tell it about other people.

Virginia Woolf

In those situations we need to take time for some reflection, seek feedback that we really attend to, and open ourselves up to see things from a different perspective. Perhaps at times like these we need what the Buddhists refer to as a *kalyana mitra*, or "noble friend," who as John O'Donahue[3] tells us in <u>Anam Cara</u> "will not accept pretension but will gently and firmly confront you with your own blindness."

What "filters" or experiences of yours might occasionally get in your way of knowing what's really going on?

What might you do to eliminate or reduce those filters?

How might you practice more "presence" in your organization or environment?

Authenticity requires being awake to what's going on inside – self-awareness, as well as to external reality. Often leadership consists largely of seeing what's ahead, seeing things first, or seeing things more clearly than others; Max DePree, retired CEO of Hermann-Miller, said that a "leader's first job is to define reality." Steve Jobs and Apple Computer were the first to see the potential for small, powerful personal computers when IBM and larger mainstream computer manufacturers only saw limited market potential. IBM's limited visibility could have been partially due to blindness that stemmed from its prior success, (Amazingly, IBM did quite well for a number of years despite Thomas J. Watson – the Board Chairman's view in 1943 that "there is a world market for only about five computers!")

You must never confuse faith that you will prevail in the end - which you can never afford to lose - with the discipline to confront the most brutal facts of your current reality, whatever they might be.
Jim Stockdale

As Mark Twain said: "It isn't what we don't know that gives us trouble, it's what we know for sure that just ain't so." Humorous, but of course unfortunate for those who lost out on account of things they knew that in fact weren't so; examples abound. A classic is the Decca Recording Company executive in 1962 who said as he turned away the Beatles: "We don't like their sound, and groups of guitars are on their way out." Another is the American automobile company executive who, in the August 2nd, 1968 issue of *Business Week*, declared: "With over fifty foreign cars already on sale here, the Japanese auto industry isn't likely to carve out a big slice of the U.S. market for itself." More recent and more painful for many, were Alan Greenspan and the Federal Reserve's pre-2008 misreading of the housing bubble and of the systematic risks undertaken by big banking.

At Croton Point in the Hudson River, about forty miles north of New York City, recreational and commercial vessels stay well clear of Potato Rock, a granite spur that at low tide has been known to gash hulls and damage many props. What's interesting is that Potato Rock no longer exists, despite being clearly marked as a navigational hazard on charts for the area; it was blasted away long ago by the U.S. Coast Guard and Corps of Engineers.

For twenty years or so, mariners have dutifully maneuvered around a non-existent navigational hazard; they were influenced by its reputation and paid close attention to their navigational charts, which as it turns out haven't been updated since Potato Rock's demolition. Often it's best not to rely on any single source of intelligence. Again, we have to remember that "the map isn't the territory."

Of course the worst kind of navigational error at sea is steaming ahead on a pre-ordained course and running into things we assume are not there or don't notice – like rocks, icebergs or other vessels. A classic tragic case is the loss of over 1,500 lives when the Titanic sank off the Newfoundland coast in 1912. She was steaming at near full speed when she grazed an iceberg that wasn't spotted, and went down in a little over three hours. There wasn't much worry about icebergs since the Titanic was supposed to be "unsinkable;" besides, they had a schedule to keep.

Mountain climbers talk about comparable disasters in their world caused by "summit fever" – a mad drive to accomplish a goal or reach the top that blinds climbers to ominous dangers. You might say that many of the investment banks that toppled with the demise of the real estate market were victimized – or more accurately victimized untold others – on account of "summit fever."

The worst recorded naval disaster was the loss of nearly two thousand British seamen, including the fleet's Commodore, when all three of the fleet's ships struck rock and sank off the coast of Scilly in 1707. Navigational errors – specifically, incorrect calculation of longitude, likely compounded by bad weather and visibility, caused the disaster. Ironically, although never confirmed, records later retrieved indicated that earlier in the voyage the fleet's commander had a common seaman hanged for insubordination; he had questioned the navigational judgment of a senior officer. Likely there were seamen aboard with very practical knowledge of the waters – more accurate than their commanding officers' – who later might have helped prevent the disaster. Who would have risked the noose, however, by offering it up? Not only at sea, but also in business and in life, we need to pay attention and use whatever intelligence is available to minimize unpleasant surprises and stay on course.

> *If the brutal facts are not faced by leaders, the brutal reality sets in.*
> Andy Grove

What "Potato Rocks" might there be in your life – imagined or no longer relevant hazards – that you have been avoiding and may be holding you back?

How about in your organization or where you work?

Might there be any goals or a course you are pursuing where perhaps more care is needed heeding "navigational hazards" or where you might be under the influence of "Summit Fever"?

How about in your organization or where you work?

Authentic leaders and organizations possess not only keener, but broader vision; they see the whole picture. Their view encompasses not only variables impacting short-term operations, but realities beyond their borders and time horizon. They possess a more global perspective, and a higher capacity to picture the likely impact of external developments two, three or four times removed from their immediate operations. Their broader view also enables them to project the impact of their own decisions and actions on stakeholders considerably beyond their immediate environment.

Sometimes to see things differently we need to see different things – in other words, to change our perspective. We can see more of what there is to see and of the big picture by stepping away from where or how we usually view things. Executives, for example, learn more about what's really true in their organizations by walking around and seeing things from the perspectives of those on the floor or in the field;

Seeing the world through the largest number of lenses makes it unlikely that some new reality will appear without being aware of it at all.
Robert Theobald

citizens of developed, democratic nations can learn more about freedom and the true effects of poverty by traveling abroad.

In the 1991 movie *The Doctor,* William Hurt played the eponymous character of "the doctor who knew it all until he became a patient." After a brutal attack that left him incapacitated, he learned first-hand what it was like to experience the helplessness and depersonalization that patients often experience in clinics and hospitals.

Artists see things differently than business people, and if paying attention, each can be enriched by the other's perspectives and see new possibilities. Engineers see thing differently than marketing executives, sales managers see things differently than accountants, university professors see things differently than administrators, etc., and unfortunately often see right past each other.

Sensing the whole picture means giving attention to all dimensions of who we are – body, mind, emotions and spirit. Anyone who claims or acts like emotions including hurt, sadness, envy or anger have no place in business is not dealing with reality. Reality is that they are present whether or not we acknowledge them; we need to deal with them sooner or later, and it will be less costly if we pay attention to them from the start.

As much as they may appear so, pre and post-merger "integration" discussions are not the rational exercises they are often made out to be. The players in those situations have personal needs, hopes and fears that we ignore at our peril; often those needs are disguised as rational arguments around how to integrate operations. Truly authentic conversations that openly acknowledge and explore those needs, hopes and fears lead to the best and most sustainable paths forward.

Discerning the truth or what's really going on is a "team sport." Authentic leaders need to not only have the courage of their own convictions, but the courage to have their convictions challenged. As the economist and futurist Robert Theobald said: "Seeing the world through the largest possible number of lenses makes it unlikely that some reality will occur without us being aware of it at all." We all bring different perspectives, filters and points of view to whatever we see or hear, and the truest picture will integrate the views from all "lenses."

Authentic leaders and authentic organizations engage in dialog; they invite and empower different points of view, and create forums for exchanging those points of view in the interest of keener vision and better decisions. We will talk more about dialog in Chapters Four and Six, but for now know that it is different than discussion, or when we are often more interested in making a point than learning.

Dialog is an open conversation where the intent is to truly explore and learn from alternate points of view in hopes of getting closer to "the truth," the reality of what's really going on or the best course of action. Too often we have discussions where despite the appearance of interest in hearing and learning from others' perspectives, they become forums for promoting our own viewpoints. Conversation that merely feigns interest in others' points of view and creates the impression that they count only smoothes the way to foregone conclusions.

> *The pursuit of truth is like picking raspberries. You miss a lot if you approach it from only one angle.*
> Randal Marlin

One client with a history of rocky relations between two groups structured opportunities for the groups to interact and at least called them what they really were: "opinion exchange" meetings. I think what mainly transpired was just that: <u>exchanges</u> of opinions versus learning or softening of positions informed by others' points of view. This was an institution that had truly been suffering from a "hardening of the categories" over the years.

TRUTH-TELLING

Seeing the truth or reality of what's really going on is only half the battle. Authentic leaders are also *truth-tellers* who "call them as they see them" and voice "inconvenient truths." Did you ever wonder how many problems would be avoided or resolved more quickly if we simply told the truth? Think of the negative impact on performance, potential, careers, motivation and organization cultures just from inability or unwillingness to tell the truth in performance appraisals. Or, have you ever been in a meeting with your boss or perhaps your boss' boss where the boss asks for frank criticism of his or her idea that everyone believes is destined for failure? How frank was the criticism? If there was none and the idea was implemented, how did it go? What happens when we are told that a process will be an open one for making an important decision but it turns out that we are just going through the motions because a decision has already been made?

From my observations, even when that happens just once, and certainly if it happens more often, it is difficult and sometimes almost impossible to restore trust; institutional memories are long and strong.

> *Morality in government begins with officials using words as honestly as possible to describe the truth.*
> David Gergen

Most of us have chosen to not tell the truth or whole truth at one time or another. Sometimes that's the best decision, but that decision needs to be reached with care and in the best interest of all parties, not just for our own convenience.

We need to tell ourselves the truth about not telling the truth. Sometimes we think it doesn't matter if "no one is the wiser," but truth usually finds its way out one way or another. (As Mark Twain said: "If you tell the truth you don't need to have as good a memory!")

Sometimes we do not tell the truth because we don't trust ourselves or lack the skills to do it well. Sometimes it is not so much a skills issue, but one that requires more courage – a topic covered in more depth in Chapter Six. Any organization or relationship would benefit from more "courageous conversations" – where all parties share their truths as authentically and skillfully as they are able in the interest of growth and advancing the organization or relationships. (Note: "as skillfully as they are able and in the interest of growth and advancing the organization" is very different from "venting," "brutal honesty" or "letting it all out" without regard for consequences.)

Authentic leaders and authentic organizations cultivate truth-telling cultures. In truth-telling cultures all know that they share responsibility for communicating openly, sharing bad news quickly, voicing disagreements, soliciting contrary or unpopular opinions and engaging in courageous conversations. In a truth-telling culture it would

> *The truth - you've got to deal with it or it will kill you bit by bit.*
> Ziggy Marley

not have been possible for engineers at Thiokol to remain silent about concerns that an "o-ring" could be faulty; that faulty "o-ring" was the main contributing factor to explosion of the *Challenger* space shuttle that killed seven astronauts in 1986.

Truth-telling would have gone a long way in averting or minimizing the 2008 economic collapse due to organizational cultures that discouraged questioning the numbers or assumptions. To cite just one of many examples, in June, 2008, a fourteen-year Lehman Brothers veteran was fired for raising a red flag with the securities' firm auditor about $50 billion of assets that had been transferred off Lehman's balance sheet. All would be better off now had "canaries in the coal mine" like her been nurtured instead of punished.

Good leaders cultivate honest speech; they love advisors who tell them the truth.

Proverbs 16: 13

The Message Bible

If we want truth-telling cultures we must model truth-telling, beginning with acknowledging and telling the truth first to ourselves. We must drag "inconvenient truths" from dark corners so they can benefit from the light of examination and discussion. We must find the courage and develop our skills to stand up for what we believe and to send clear, unmixed messages about decisions and actions that we believe are right, those we believe are wrong, and why.

We must not only have the courage of our convictions, but the courage to have our convictions challenged. No matter how convinced we may be that our opinion or planned course is correct, we must be willing to really hear alternate points of view and to engage in genuine dialog. As leaders, to build truth-telling cultures, we must state our expectation that seeking and telling the truth is everyone's responsibility.

Most important, we must empower and reinforce truth-telling behaviors, and reward those who have the courage to speak truth to power. We must be ever vigilant against sending the message intentionally or unintentionally that speaking up could be career limiting. We need to coach and provide others with the resources they need to find their voices and engage in skillful courageous conversations.

Are there any "inconvenient truths" you're aware of that could benefit from some light of day?

What conversation would be good for you, or for your organization, to have that you're not having now?

TRANSPARENCY

In the words of Mother Theresa: "Honesty and transparency make you vulnerable; be honest and transparent anyway." Transparency pays multiple dividends: Especially given today's electronic and connected world, information that before we maybe had the option for keeping to ourselves will likely find the light of day sooner or later. Proactively sharing information about things like suppliers, potential or real product flaws or our motivations and rationale for potentially unpopular decisions builds our credibility and trustworthiness with customers, employers, partners and the public.

Further, recognizing and openly acknowledging mistakes or problems gives us the opportunity and incentive to correct problems early and before we may be forced to correct them (in ways not of our own choosing) by external parties. Operating transparently also builds a kind of "governor" or self-regulating mechanism to help us monitor and determine the correctness, fairness and likely impact of our decisions and actions. As I write this it is still uncertain what Toyota knew or when they knew it about any faulty braking

Who is more foolish, the child afraid of the dark or the man afraid of the light?
Maurice Freehill

mechanisms that contributed to the recall of millions of vehicles and potentially to accident casualties. Whatever lasting damage is done to Toyota's reputation and market share, however, will likely hinge more on any discoveries around lack of transparency than on automotive design or manufacturing problems themselves.

Knowing that a decision or action may be scrutinized by others helps us scrutinize it ourselves more thoroughly than we otherwise might and adjust our course for the better. One of the best ways I know to evaluate the ethics of decisions and actions in advance is to imagine (realistically these days, to <u>assume</u>) that it will be in tomorrow's news. Would we be okay with that? Why or why not? How would the news be greeted by our various stakeholders or constituencies? Anticipating the reactions and consequences, is there anything we would do differently?

When I worked in Human Resources I always had difficulty with my employers' reluctance to post or discuss pay ranges for jobs. I assumed that the external market and competitors had likely pieced together most of the picture anyway, and suspected that the main rationale was to prevent employees from questioning the fairness of who got paid what. Ranges for the most part were market-driven, and "fair" or not, I believed that people might as well know how things worked. I believed (and still do) that open conversations about pay levels could arm and motivate staff to make better-informed career decisions, reduce idle speculation and suspicions, improve credibility and trust of leadership, and likely lead to a few deserved adjustments in pay.

The "whole-mindedness" of integrity includes assuming responsibility and transparency regarding the impact of our decisions and actions, however far removed from our immediate spheres. A product's "story" – including origins of manufacture, working conditions, suppliers and environmental impact – is becoming an increasingly important factor in buyers' and workers' decisions about the kind of organizations they want to be associated with.

Organizations that openly share positive stories about how they operate and their products are better positioned to compete in markets where consumers, employees and potential employees desire to be better stewards. A 2007 Monster-TRAK.com study revealed that 80% of young professionals are interested in securing work that has a positive impact on the environment, and that 92% would prefer working for an organization that is environmentally friendly.

AUTHENTICITY AND ACTION

Meeting the *Authenticity* challenge requires that leaders answer the question: Leadership for what?" In The Leader As Servant, Robert Greenleaf describes leaders as servants first – they foresee the needs of others and take the initiative to act in service to others and the community. As Dag Hammarskjold stated: "In our world, the road to holiness necessarily passes through the world of action." We cannot be leaders if we see and do not act, and leaders at their best empower others to act in service to a noble purpose.

True and sustainable leadership is not power over, but power with – inspiring and empowering others to act in pursuit of worthy goals. I have a favorite scene in the movie *Braveheart,* depicting the Scots' struggle for

> *There can be no happiness if the things we believe in are different than the things we do.*
>
> Freya Stark

freedom from English rule. A rag-tag band of Scottish farmers and peasants find themselves facing a British army vastly superior in number, armament and skills. Scottish noblemen, in the game primarily to enhance their land holdings, attempt to rally the ragtag band, but their voices carry little authority.

As the outnumbered and fearful farmers and peasants begin to disperse, grumbling "this is not our fight," the noblemen plead with them to stay at least long enough to negotiate with the English army generals. Enter John Wallace

> *All worthwhile men have good thoughts, good ideas and good intentions – but precious few of them ever translate those into action.*
>
> John Hancock Field

(played by Mel Gibson,) who charges to the front line in war paint with his band of "freedom fighters." John Wallace then truly rallies the assembly – trumping their fear by tapping a deep-seated need

they all experienced to live lives of freedom and meaning – or to die knowing they did all in their power to attain it.

And he was honest: "Die – yes, many of you will, but some of you will live long lives; live or die you will go to your graves as free men!" Wallace articulated a cause worthy of making the ultimate sacrifice for; the genuineness of his message, coupled with his willingness to sacrifice his own life in service to the cause, rallied the outnumbered band to defeat the English on that battlefield and ultimately win freedom for Scotland.

Herbert Hoover was right when he said, "Words without action are the assassins of idealism." To navigate the *Authenticity* challenge successfully we need to say what we mean and "match our deeds with our creed."

What action can you begin to take now that will right some wrong or meet some need that you are aware of?

What might you do to empower others to act in service to a noble purpose or in pursuit of a worthy goal?

AUTHENTICITY – KEY POINTS

Meeting the *Authenticity* challenge requires *trueness*, *truthfulness* and *transparency*. Leaders and organizations must be true to their mission and values and take care to walk their talk. They must above all be truthful with themselves and acutely aware of what is happening around them, including any "inconvenient truths" that need to see the light of day. Leaders and organizations of integrity create truth-telling cultures and model transparency, knowing that is essential for fostering trust and sustaining long-term successful relationships with employees, customers and stakeholders.

Like first-rate scientists, effective leaders operate with the philosophy that the pursuit of truth is more important than its possession. They have not only the courage of their convictions but also the courage to have their convictions challenged, and are not fearful of true dialog that will help everyone learn.

To be authentic means taking and empowering action that is consistent with beliefs and purpose. Authentic leadership reflects the belief that the purpose of leaders is to serve – to cause action and equip those they serve to accomplish noble ends.

A man's true greatness lies in the consciousness of an honest purpose in life, founded on a just estimate of himself and everything else, on frequent self-examinations, and a steady obedience to the rule which he knows to be right, without troubling himself about what others may think or say, or whether they do or do not do that which he thinks and says and does.
Marcus Aurelius

CHAPTER 4 | *ALIGNMENT*

> *Civilizations should be measured by the degree of diversity attained and the degree of unity retained.*
> W.H. Auden

> *It is hard to get someone to understand something when their salary depends on them not understanding it.*
> Upton Sinclair

> *A modern view of the processes of growth, decay and renewal must give due emphasis to both continuity and change in human institutions.*
> John W. Gardner

I like this inscription on one of my favorite art museum's exterior walls: "Bits And Pieces Brought Together To Provide Some Semblance Of A Whole.¹" To me it speaks of *alignment* – connecting elements in some fashion that tells a story, reinforces a theme or supports a purpose – as in "architectural integrity." We recognize architectural integrity when a structure is compelling, its purpose is clear and elements don't clash; we experience a kind of "harmony," and everything seems to fit. Going back to our tapestry analogy in Chapter Two, leaders and organizations of integrity weave "tapestries of intention" – leader behaviors and organizational systems as well as practices all seem to fit and reinforce their purpose, values and aims.

Over lunch recently a business owner revealed some of the threads in his and his business' tapestry of intentions: Many owners and CEOs, this one included, say that they want workers to "act like owners." Congruent with my lunch partner's intentions, he established the practice several years ago of dividing up the firm's profits each year for distribution to everyone in the company

Great things are not done by impulse, but by a series of things brought together.
Vincent van Gogh

As a result, the employees really do feel and act like owners, collaborating over the last few years on decisions and changes in processes that have significantly improved overall profits. Further, the owner's decision to share profits reinforced his aims for an equitable and collaborative work environment as well as his personal stated purpose "to enrich the lives of others."

He enriches their lives in other ways as well: Rather than accepting a prestigious industry award himself at an out-of-state ceremony as other organizations' executives typically did, he asked the most senior worker from his company to take the trip and accept the award.

Compensation, rewards and recognition – monetary or otherwise – exert the potentially strongest "errant threads" in some organizations' tapestries of intention. I still remember an article by Frederick Herzberg early in my career entitled: *On The Folly Of Expecting X And Paying Y.* It warned against compensation schemes that reinforce behaviors or outcomes contrary to what we hope for. A classic example is hoping for profitable sales and customer retention, but compensating sales personnel for total sales only, with no pay adjustments for returns or customer dissatisfaction. Another is extolling the value and desirability of teamwork but compensating only for individual achievement, where any time collaborating on joint goals takes away from potential individual compensation.

One manufacturing organization I know of displayed many of the posters and slogans we've seen encouraging teamwork and listed "Collaboration" among its core values. I guess one of the "collaborative" opportunities was for engineers in design and production teams to rate one another as part of their annual performance appraisal process, which – you guessed it, quickly became a zero-sum game that eroded any semblance of trust. The stakes and undesirable consequences mushroomed when the organization used team performance ratings as the primary determinant of whom to cut whenever they "rightsized." As you might imagine, no amount of exhortations to collaborate or teambuilding efforts could overcome the rating system and its consequences in terms of what people paid attention to.

> *He that gives good advice builds with one hand; he that gives good counsel and example builds with both; but he that gives good admonition and bad example builds with one hand and tears down with the other.*
>
> Francis Bacon

Washington Mutual, or "WaMu," was seized by the federal government in September of 2008 and was the largest U.S. bank failure in history at that point. To a large extent, its demise was the product of a loan underwriting culture that was terribly misaligned with what loan underwriting functions are supposed to be. A *New York Times*[2] article shortly after the bank's failure described a culture that was clearly about the *quantity* and not the *quality* of loans that WaMu could process. There was intense pressure to meet aggressive goals for underwriting new mortgages, which coupled with compensation, incentives and personnel practices sent a very clear message that it was all about volume.

A loan officer featured in the article had on many occasions tried to reject flawed and even fraudulent loan applications, only to be reprimanded, written up and eventually let go. On the other hand, peer loan officers who operated by different standards and approved shaky loans were regularly rewarded with exotic trips and promotions. Little attention was paid when loans that were initially rejected but later approved defaulted, and troubling signs of accelerating defaults were virtually ignored.

Hiring systems – either whom or how we hire – can also reinforce or take away from what we hope to be or achieve. A while back I read about a manufacturer of children's playground equipment that keeps teeter totters, slides and other playground equipment in its lobby; only job candidates that look the equipment over and maybe even try it out get invited back for second interviews. A friend recently participated in a group interview process to be considered for employment as an attendant with one of the "friendly airlines." Part of the experience was for candidates to share something about themselves with the group that reflected who they are. Not only was that an effective tool for getting to know candidates, but it reinforced the airline's belief in the importance of building relationships with customers and coworkers. From day one, these kinds of interviewing and hiring practices signal and reinforce organizations' cultures and send clear messages about their missions and expectations.

Training and development provide further opportunities to reinforce (or not) an organization's purpose, strategies, desired culture and expectations. Consistent and adequate investments in education and development at all levels help make sentiments like "people are our greatest asset" believable.

In lean times, consistently cutting first the training and development budgets sends an opposite message. Defining only technical education and not team or personal development experiences as "job related" and therefore reimbursable sends a message – intended or not, that team and communication skills may not be that important. A CEO's and senior leaders' personal involvement in design and delivery of management education reinforces the importance of leadership development and the organization's intention to develop its management and supervisory ranks. Their involvement also more than likely shapes development experiences so they are aligned with an organization's desired culture, strategies and senior leaders' expectations.

Organizational design, including formality, levels of supervision, groupings of functions, and authority granted is a critical arena to align with desired culture and aims. Both formal organization structures – organizational charts, position descriptions and the like, and informal organization structures – including how functions interact and how they connect, require attention. Rigid reporting relationships and protocols, for example, will for the most part counter an organization's intent to open up communication or improve innovation. In one organizational restructuring project, the director of human resources role was made a vice presidential position reporting directly to the president instead of to a vice president of administration. The role and reporting level change was better aligned with the organization's realization that human resources systems and development would play an even greater role in its future competitiveness. Simply encouraging my clients to consciously and conscientiously articulate design criteria – what they desire their organizational structure to accomplish – helps assure more structural integrity and that form will in fact follow function.

Measurement, information collected and feedback provided – or not (addressed in the next chapter on *Accountability*) also send strong messages about what really counts. What gets measured and rewarded is usually what gets attention and

> *The activities and behavior of people at every level must be aligned with the main thing. When this happens tremendous organizational power is created.*
> George Labovitz
> and Victor Rosansky[2]

what gets done. For example, if our intent is to differentiate ourselves by providing the best customer service, we will not succeed if we do not make feedback on customer service a priority. If our intent is to diversify our workforce, then we need to collect information about efforts to recruit diverse employees, experiences of diverse hires on the job and themes of exit interviews when diverse employees leave.

What gets recognized and rewarded, whom and how we hire, education and training, organizational structure and what gets measured are critical levers that organizations can deploy to assure alignment with what is most important. Organizations must be careful not to build up with one hand and tear down with the other; their best intentions, like stock, lose value when little backs them up.

The same can be said for leaders. Do others view our lives as "tapestries of intention"? Do our behaviors and how we allocate our time and treasure "create some semblance of a whole" and fit with our stated aims and values?

As a leader . . . (It would be useful to solicit the views of a few trusted friends on this one.)

What behaviors and practices reinforce or fit your purpose, core values and aims?

What behaviors and practices do not reinforce or fit your purpose, core values and aims?

Are there any changes to how you allocate your time and treasure, or other adjustments that would create more "semblance of a whole" in your life or work?

What systems and practices in your organization reinforce its stated purpose, values and aims? How?

Pay, recognition and rewards:

How and whom you hire:

Education and development:

Organizational structure:

Information, measures and feedback:

Other:

What systems and practices in your organization do not reinforce your mission and values or might send "mixed messages" about what's really important?

Becoming the best that we can be requires that we attend not only to *alignment* the noun, but to *aligning* the verb. *Alignment* is about reinforcing enduring missions, values and aims; *aligning* means learning, adaptation, growth and change. Chameleons get a bad rap, as when we call someone a "chameleon" that appears to change his opinion or point of view too readily. I admire chameleons, though; they have a knack for adapting or blending into their environment without giving up their "chameleon-ness." Saint Benedict, a sixth-century monk, was more elegant and profound when he characterized the difference between "stabilitas" – what is foundational and must not change, with "conversatio" – what should remain "in conversation" and open for change while still preserving the foundation.

> *Life is the continuous adjustment of internal relations to external relations.*
> Herbert Spencer

Shoot ahead to the twentieth century, and Jim Collins research demonstrated how the same dynamic accounted for significantly higher and more sustainable organizational performance. Organizations that both adhered to their *core ideology* ("stabilitas") and maintained *adaptive mechanisms* ("conversatio") delivered significantly higher returns.

Integrity is a dance; being our best and staying in the game require inflexibility around fundamental aims and values <u>and</u> flexibility around everything else. We need to not only "walk the talk" but "dance the dance." We need to heed Benjamin Disraeli's counsel that "the secret to success is constancy of purpose" as well as Will Rogers': "Even if you are on the right track you'll get run over if you just sit there."

Examples abound for organizations in all industries that failed at aligning (the verb) by not adapting to, or even seeing, new or evolving technical, economic, regulatory, social or competitive trends.

In <u>Balanced Brand</u>, John Foley[4] makes the point that "When your corporate values are out of alignment with stakeholder values, trouble is right around the corner." Nike was caught off guard when it discovered too late how much Americans cared about working conditions where Nike shoes are manufactured. Wal-Mart was thrown off course when it learned late in the game that a significant share of shoppers care a great deal about fair working conditions and pay in addition to just everyday low prices. It seems these days that almost every industry and organization is catching on quite quickly to the fact that it will be out of luck if it cannot demonstrate alignment with "green" values and concern for the environment. Some organizations are also learning that beyond customers, potential customers and shareholders, other important groups of stakeholders need to be taken into account In his book <u>Authentic Leadership</u>[5], Medtronic's former CEO

> *We must adjust to changing times and still hold to unchanging principles.*
>
> Jimmy Carter

> *To separate the purpose of a business from the purpose of people who are in the business is, I think, not a good thing.*
>
> Michael Josephson

describes how putting employees and customers ahead of shareholders' interests is what accounted for Medtronic's success – including increased shareholder value in the end.

Alignment includes the capacity to "harmonize" – ideas, opinions, cultures – and in the case of mergers and accompanying integration efforts, whole organizations. Alignment means unity, not sameness; the poet W. H. Auden said that a successful measure of true harmonization is "the degree of diversity attained and the degree of unity retained."

Alignment necessarily begins with differences, and when handled well ends with decisions, solutions and outcomes superior to any that would have been possible without diversity. For communities and organizations, as with nature, diversity can be a source of competitive advantage; it is the wellspring of different perspectives, methods, ideas and capabilities that fuels innovation and adaptability. Capitalizing on the potential benefits of diversity requires environments that respect differences and abilities to leverage them.

> *Unity, not uniformity, must be our aim. We attain unity only through variety. Differences must be integrated.*
>
> Mary Parker Follett

Most important is to actively seek, cultivate and encourage diverse perspectives and assure that we are truly listening, especially if we disagree or initially don't understand a contrary opinion or approach.

We sometimes confuse listening with agreement without realizing that we always have the option of not agreeing after really listening. We might learn something that alters our point of view and leads to better outcomes; even if not, truly listening (not faking it) is one of the best vehicles for building ownership and acceptance of whatever is decided. Truly listening and demonstrating real openness to others' points of view are also among the strongest ways to build relationships and trust.

One tool for creating unity from differences is *dialog,* which we introduced in Chapter Three. Dialog requires that we at least initially suspend any judgment of "good" and "bad" ideas or of "right" and "wrong" approaches, and that we not rush to a conclusion. Unlike *discussion* where often we make our best arguments to convince others about the merits of our points of view, with *dialog* our sole purpose is to purely *understand* different or contrary points of view and to learn without reaching any decisions or conclusions.

Attempting to purely understand others or contrary perspectives – what others see, why others believe what they do, what assumptions they are making and how they formed opinions – without judgment or intentions of "carrying the day" – expands the total intelligence available, and ultimately a group's options, before deciding or acting. Dialog is one of the core competencies of "learning organizations" that Peter Senge[6] wrote about and that we will revisit in Chapter Six.

Margaret Fuller, the early nineteenth-century journalist and women's rights activist, reminded us that unity can exist with differences, provided that those differences are governed by the same key note. That is why agreement and alignment around a shared purpose or mission, common aims and core values are critical.

> *Harmony exists in difference no less than in likeness, if only the same key note govern both parts.*
>
> Margaret Fuller

Our motives must be "pure in heart," so to speak, if we

are to have "fair fights" over methods and means. As Jim Collins[7] put it in <u>Good To Great</u>, we must start out by "getting the right people on (and the wrong people off) the bus." The "right people" are those in tune with the purpose of the trip (mission) and how you wish to travel (values).

One client is now the merger of two organizations that were originally on opposite ends – east and west – of a large metropolitan community. In a recent conversation, an executive of the merged organization relayed stories of

Diversity is an unyielding fact of our time. If quickened by fear it divides; if quickened by hope it unites.
Robert W. Terry

the skirmishes that took place among units of the east and west contingents – typical in newly merged organizations – over which systems, methods and practices, in this case the "east's" or the "west's" would prevail.

His message to the warring parties was: "Don't choose east or west, but what's best!" – best for the customer, best for business and best for the now united organization. His short, poetic bit of coaching is a wonderful way to capture what real "integration" is all about – not one way or the other because "that's yours" and "this is mine," but what way is most congruent with our now shared purpose and values. I am convinced this young executive will go far.

Another client, with operations in two cities separated only by a river, pointed out that while the river is a boundary of sorts that separates, it also connects the two communities. Rivers, like other features of nature that are simultaneously boundaries and connectors, play important roles in ecosystems. Marshes separate lakes from dry ground and also connect them; deltas separate land from sea and also connect them; plains separate yet connect fields and forests and so on.

Boundaries, or connectors, within ecosystems are mediums for transferring materials and energy, moderating temperatures and aiding migration from one region to another; that can be true for organizations as well. Those inhabiting "marginal roles" in organizations, communities or cultures can also play important aligning, or harmonizing, roles transferring "nutrients" – energy and ideas – across boundaries.

Those deeply embedded in particular systems, philosophies or communities often have difficulty seeing or learning from others with different perspectives; as the jazz great Don Cherry put it: "When people believe in boundaries, they become part of them." Political parties or ideologies like "red" and "blue" states or the "Tea Party" and liberals are classical cases in point. In my home state there are often sharply different perspectives and consequently barriers to understanding between residents of metropolitan communities and those who live in rural areas. Examples also abound across organizational units like sales and accounting, administration and faculty or manufacturing and quality control. "Aligning" the verb involves bridging across different philosophies, systems or units to engage in dialog, facilitate learning and exchange energy and

Alignment is the essence of management.

Fred Smith, Chairman FedEx

ideas across boundaries; that is true integration and what "harmonizing" is about. People and groups in "marginal" or boundary-spanning capacities can play unique roles as bridges across ideological and organizational boundaries.

Think of a potentially controversial decision or course of action where your mind is pretty well made up; who can you think of that might disagree with your decision or course of action?

What benefit might there be engaging in real dialog with any who see things differently than you on this matter? How will you make that happen? (See Chapter Six for tips on dialog.)

What philosophies, organizational units, communities or factions are you aware of that could benefit from some "bridging?" How can you facilitate that?

Alignment is about connecting. External connections help keep us attuned to the world, our market and others around us; internal connections organizationally unite people, plans, systems and behaviors to serve our constituency and fulfill our mission. Too often, on account of overly aggressive growth, attempts to reduce costs or efforts to increase efficiencies we overlook these important internal connections.

My internet cable service is provided by an operation that was acquired a few years ago by a much larger cable and entertainment distributor; I pay a fairly healthy amount each month to that distributor for web-hosting, internet and e-mail service. Recently, when I could receive no e-mail, I called the phone number for technical support listed on my monthly cable bill. As it turns out, they are not the ones who provide technical support for my system, so they referred me to technical support for the outfit I originally signed up for that they had acquired. (Are you still with me?)

That technical support operation said they were aware of the problem but could do nothing about it. Apparently the trouble was caused by a new spam filter installed by – you guessed it – yet a third entity that acquired the original company I called! They at least gave me a phone number for that conglomerate's technical support, but it turned out to be a wrong number. Luckily the problem worked itself out after a few hours. Does this sound familiar?

Another common occurrence of "the back bone not connected to the hip bone . . . not connected to the leg bone, etc." syndrome is a variation of attempting to resolve computer glitches when you call the computer manufacturer who states emphatically that it is a software problem; of course when we then call the software provider, we are told emphatically that it is a hardware issue. And the whole scenario gets more complicated when we are also crossing language and culture lines while attempting to resolve a problem.

My view is that if a computer comes packaged with particular software and whatever other components, for the product to have *integrity* – where everything is connected, then service should be part of the package deal. I think that even if that kind of seamlessness or product / service integrity costs more in the short run many would be willing to pay the price and it would become a significant competitive advantage in the long run.

Often the internal connections required for delivering as

promised are lacking because some workers in the organization have too small a view of why they are really there. They do not identify with larger end goals, but instead view their work strictly through their own or their particular function's lens. We've come to call this the "silo effect," where there may be much intense activity within the boundaries and for the benefit of separate units, but where little connects them.

Over the years we've made much progress breaking down such silos by analyzing value chains, executing quality improvement initiatives and adopting process improvement methodologies that cut across organizational units. In addition to continuing those efforts we need to provide the "glue" for making important connections by helping everyone focus on the whole picture – outside and inside, and on common goals. Keeping everyone focused on "the main thing" and a compelling vision helps transcend territorial and / or petty concerns.

> *We are apt to forget that we are only one of a team, that in unity there is strength and that we are strong only as long as each unit in our organization functions with precision.*
> Samuel Tilden

As you think about a product or service that you are part of providing, where might there be any "disconnects" or factors interfering with delivery of the product or service as promised? (Obviously,

your customers or those next in line who receive your product or service are in the best position to help you answer this question.)

What are steps you can take to identify or validate where those "disconnects" exist and resolve them?

There is much talk and concern about organizational or functional "silos," but little awareness of the degree to which we have "siloed" our physical, mental, emotional and spiritual lives. Often we lose sight of entire dimensions of who we are, focusing on only one or two and subsequently falling short of all that we can be. Some of us seek fulfillment and attempt to excel in all the wrong places, or at least in only some of the right places. To bring all of who we are to life and work, we need to be in touch with all of who we are – physically, mentally, emotionally and spiritually.

Since the Newtonian age, especially in Western culture, the physical and mental realms of our work and work lives have prevailed. We often distrust, discount or simply ignore much of what is not tangible or what we cannot rationalize scientifically. We can fall prey to measuring the worth of our work solely

> *All true educators since the time of Socrates and Plato have agreed that the primary object of education is the attainment of inner harmony, or, to put it into more up-to-date language, the integration of the personality. Without such integration learning is no more than a collection of scraps, and the accumulation of knowledge becomes a danger to mental health.*
>
> Sir Alfred Zimmern

by what we can exchange for it – bigger houses, faster cars or nicer clothes. Our default solutions for organizational challenges often involve variations of juggling assets or physically moving around boxes on organization charts.

We went through a brief period in the '90s when it was safe in some circles to talk about business and spirit in the same breath, but as the pace quickened and markets became even more competitive, we quickly got over that. Most mainstream businesses traditionally downplayed the role of emotions at work until Daniel Goleman[8] demonstrated powerful connections between "emotional intelligence," or "E.Q.," and performance.

A 2006 study by Mercer Delta Consulting and The Economist Intelligence Unit[9] concluded that "whole leaders in possession not only of cognitive skills but emotional intelligence and strong values – head, heart and 'guts' – will be what's needed to tackle increasingly complex global business challenges." The study also concluded that such "whole leaders" are in short supply, and that organizations able to accelerate leaders' growth in all dimensions, especially "heart" and "guts" competencies, will gain competitive advantage.

To be whole and to meet the alignment challenge at a personal level, we need to find work that meets not only our material needs and provides sufficient mental challenge, but that is a fit emotionally and that has meaning for us.

Slow down and enjoy life. It's not only the scenery you miss by going too fast – you also miss the sense of where you are going and why.
Eddie Cantor

We experience holes in our work and lives because we never really appreciated what it means to be whole. I never liked the reference to a "work / life balance;" it implies a need to juggle and compromise, or to live "separate but equal" work and personal lives. "Alignment" or "harmony" seems to better capture what we need, where we are not settling for trade-offs or living one life and then another, but where we are truly attaining congruency and weaving "tapestries of intentions" whole-cloth.

As we know, trees that best survive storms are those with the deepest, most firmly grounded roots and flexible branches. We can learn a lot from trees – we too, as well as organizations, need to have roots that are firmly grounded and we need to be flexible. We need to be grounded by our values, principles and purpose as

> *We cannot become what we need to be by remaining what we are.*
>
> Max De Pree

well as demonstrate flexibility and openness interacting with the world in pursuit of our aims. You may have noticed that some of us and some organizations make very odd, endangered "trees" by reversing the whole thing: surface-deep, flabby roots coupled with rigidity in our approach to the world and suffering from a "hardening of the categories."

To stretch the analogy further, some trees are rather lopsided, bearing only one or two strong main branches, and others are full and round with multiple main branches stemming from their trunks. If we think of main branches as the four dimensions of who we are – physical, mental, emotional and spiritual, "lop-sided" leaders and organizations are those that demonstrate growth in only one or two of those dimensions – likely physical and mental.

More "rounded out" leaders and organizations experience growth in all four dimensions; one or two do not get all of the "nutrients" or attention at the expense of the others. Just like trees, if we are to fully mature we need to remain flexible and constantly grow. Just as trees occasionally "self-prune" in the wind, we need to discard what no longer serves us to make room for new growth.

Do you feel that any of your physical, mental, emotional or spiritual dimensions may in need of attention? What are some actions you could take to increase congruence in your life or work with your

Physical needs:

Intellectual needs:

Emotional needs

Spiritual needs:

We need to grow in all dimensions of who we are to be whole "humans being." Note some conscious steps you can take to grow:

Physically:

Mentally:

Emotionally:

Spiritually:

Note some ways your organization might do an even better job of developing or accommodating these dimensions:

Physical:

Mental:

Emotional:

Spiritual:

ALIGNMENT – KEY POINTS

For leaders and their organizations, meeting the *Alignment* challenge and being our best means designing our lives and creating communities where there is a sense of "fit," or harmony.

Organizationally, "form fits function" when selection, development, rewards and other organizational systems reinforce the organization's mission, values and aims. Personally and as leaders, our words, actions and how we arrange our lives reflect "integrity of design;" there are few errant threads that interfere with the pattern in our "tapestries of intention."

> *We must adjust to changing times and still hold to unchanging principles.*
> Jimmy Carter

Alignment never ends. To be adaptable and grow means to

always be aligning. We must use our widest and highest resolution "lenses" to stay in touch with reality and remain relevant. We need to stay abreast not only of technical, scientific, economic and objective developments around us that we monitor with our heads, but also to matters of the heart. We need capacities for integrating, reconciling and harmonizing different points of view. We must value the "margins" of our cultures and those with different philosophies and points of view; those are likely sources from where the creativity and answers necessary to solve tomorrow's dilemmas will spring.

Meeting the *Alignment* challenge requires healing disconnects. The disconnects might be between stated values or intentions and behavior, organizational silos and broken processes or failure to engage all of who we are: physically, mentally, emotionally and spiritually.

CHAPTER 5 | *ACCOUNTABILITY*

> *Some favorite expressions of small children:*
> *"It's not my fault. . . They made me do it. . . I*
> *forgot." Some favorite expressions of adults:*
> *"It's not my job. . . No one told me. . . It couldn't*
> *be helped." True freedom begins and ends with*
> *personal accountability.*
>
> Dan Zadra

You don't choose the day you enter the
world and you don't choose the day you
leave. It's what you do in between that
makes all the difference.

Anita Septimus

It is not only what we do, but also what we do not do, for
which we are accountable.

Moliere

It became clear by 2008 that our economy definitely did not reflect "business at its best," and was not delivering on its promise to grow wealth, provide work or generate tax revenue for public services. Banks and bankers that promised to invest assets wisely invested instead in rotten mortgage portfolios; car companies failed to keep their promise of competitively manufacturing quality vehicles; boards did not fulfill their promise to govern soundly, and regulatory agencies neglected to exercise proper oversight. All of these failures are examples of institutions and leaders that, borrowing from Stephen Covey, failed to be accountable for "keeping the main thing the main thing."

PROMISES

Accountability means that we keep our promises. Promises come in all varieties: At the personal level we make New Year's resolutions, resolve to eat healthier, commit to saving more or promise ourselves to find better work.

At the interpersonal or relationship level we promise to be faithful and to love our partners in sickness and in health, repay a loan or show

> *Thinking well is wise;*
> *planning well, wiser; doing*
> *well wisest and best of all.*
> Persian Proverb

up at a certain time. We pledge loyalty to countries and institutions, pledge money to churches and charities and promise to fulfill the terms of contracts. Physicians take the Hippocratic Oath, and other professionals customarily make similar pledges.

Brands are implied promises; strong brands consistently meet or exceed promises that matter to their customers and stakeholders. Organizations make other kinds of promises as well, including those to meet financial projections, fulfill the terms of contracts and follow regulations. Promises made and promises kept constitute one of Accountability's cornerstones and form the foundation for trust in all domains.

> *The key to growth is to*
> *learn to make promises*
> *and to keep them.*
> Stephen R. Covey

In the first century BC, Publilius Syrus cautioned us to "never make more promises than we can keep." A first step towards fulfilling our promises is merely keeping track of the ones we make to assure that they are neither too numerous nor are too unrealistic given time available, capabilities and resources.

Like the physician we met in Chapter Three, we could all benefit by taking time periodically to review the promises we've made – today, this year or over our lives, and the degree to which we are honoring them. Self-knowledge is important here; some of us, by our nature and disposition, are more vulnerable to over-promising than others. In Chapter Two I shared that as measured by the Myers-Briggs Type Indicator, I am more inclined toward intuition than tangible facts and figures; I am also likely not as naturally organized as some with a different profile. Someone with Myers-Briggs preferences like mine, especially coupled with difficulty saying "no" and a predisposition to please others, could be vulnerable to over-promising.

We need to not only keep track of the promises we make, but also cultivate the capability to gather intelligence about the nature and difficulty of commitments that we are considering. What exactly are we committing to? What will "success" look like and who gets to decide? What or who else is involved, and will anyone be able to help? What resources are available? Has this been tried before? If we find that we have overcommitted, it may be productive to review how that happened, what questions we should have asked that we didn't and what else to do differently in the future to avoid such binds.

Take some time to review promises that you have made. Consider both work / career-related promises as well as life or relationship / family promises; also, differentiate "short," "intermediate" and "long-range" promises. "Short-range" promises may be commitments you've made that will "mature" in a few days; "intermediate-

range" promises likely have a life of a few weeks to perhaps a year (like annual work goals), and "long-range" promises are multi-year (perhaps educational goals) or life-long commitments (like "to have and to hold" or a professional oath). Are you "on course" or "off course?" Do you need to revisit any? (See "Revisiting Promises" below.)

Work / career promises
Long-range:

Intermediate-range:

Short-range:

Life or relationship / family promises
Long-range:

Intermediate-range:

Short-range:

REVISITING PROMISES

Sometimes, despite best intentions, we find that we may no longer be able to fulfill a promise or commitment; perhaps we overcommitted, reality shifts or our heart is just no longer in it. As with other ethical dilemmas, where alternate courses of action each carry pluses and minuses, we need to exercise discernment here. We will talk more about discernment, one of integrity's core capabilities, in the next chapter. In this context, discernment means first *stopping* – taking time to reflect on what promises we may not be able to keep, then *looking* – at as many dimensions of the situation, alternatives and their implications as we can, then *listening* – to our own hearts, to those affected and to others with different perspectives than our own.

Unless a capacity for thinking be accompanied by a capacity for action, a superior mind exists in torture.
Benedetto Croce

Recently I needed to decide if I would fulfill commitments that I made to a professional association. If I had not taken time to stop and give that decision some focused attention, I would have likely gotten stuck in a more reactive mode and just continued trying to respond to the demands of the commitments I made. I know from past experiences that often in those cases resentment builds up that can spill over to other arenas, and that time reacting to merely urgent demands robs attention that I should be giving other commitments of higher importance.

Taking the time to stop and reflect on our options if we've over-committed allows us to look at different dimensions of commitments that we've made, assess priorities, consider alternatives that we might not have considered, and who would be affected in what ways by whatever we decide. Then we need to listen to our own heart, perhaps find a friend or others who can weigh in, and make the best decision we can.

Dilemmas like these aren't easy, and the stakes are higher with significant life or career choices like committing to a business partnership or ending one, saying "yes" or "no" to a proposal or job offer, or ending a once significant friendship. When we have made the best decision we can, the responsible next step is to clearly communicate our decision and reasons to affected parties, and do whatever we can to help others move on (without making any more promises that we can't keep.) Imagine the impact if we were all more conscious of the commitments that we make and kept them, or if we didn't that we were honest with ourselves and others about why.

ACCOUNTABILITY AND RESPONSIBILITY

Authors of The Oz Principle[1] did a marvelous job alerting us to erosion of accountability in our culture. I agree with their assessment that part of the problem is viewing accountability as something done to or imposed on others instead of a proactive orientation to do whatever is necessary (that is legal, moral and ethical) to accomplish what needs to be done. They distinguish between individuals and organizations that get stuck in a "victimization" mind-set and those that rise above it by "seeing it, owning it, solving it and doing it."

It is easy to dodge our responsibilities, but we cannot dodge the consequences of dodging our responsibilities.
Sir Josiah Stamp

"Seeing it" requires viewing issues realistically versus hiding our heads in the sand or minimizing them; "owning it" means accepting responsibility for our contribution and doing something to resolve issues; "solving it" means finding and executing solutions to problems; "doing it" means exercising courage and resolve to act and see problems through to their resolution. It seems that too often these days individuals and institutions get trapped not only in a "victimization" mindset, but also in a blaming (or perhaps more accurately "blameless") mindset.

The secret of success is constancy to purpose.
Benjamin Disraeli

In 2006 the Highway 35W bridge that spanned the Mississippi River connecting Minneapolis and Saint Paul collapsed, killing thirteen motorists and seriously injuring dozens more. Observing the behavior of some contractors and city, county, state and federal agencies in the aftermath was a veritable character study. As with many other tragedies, including the disastrous Hurricane Katrina and terrible losses incurred by residents of New Orleans, one gets the impression that what matters most to many parties is not so much fairness for victims or a fearless search for causes to prevent future loss, but escaping with the least responsibility and blame; they neglect to "keep the main thing the main thing."

Somewhere in the missions and stated purposes of political, governmental, investigative and public service parties to disasters like the 35W bridge collapse and Hurricane Katrina is a stated or implied promise to protect citizens and treat them fairly. Integrity, and navigating the *Accountability* challenge, in situations like those requires faithfulness to their core missions and discipline to "keep their main thing their main thing." They need to cease efforts to shift blame and responsibility and strengthen their resolve to "see it, own it, solve it and do it."

Success is more permanent when you achieve it without destroying your principles.
Walter Cronkite

Organizations and leaders that responsibly embody "see it, own it, solve it and do it" are the ones we trust as workers and consumers. One positive example I remember in my home state is Schwan's, the largest home-delivery food company in the United States. In 1994 nearly a quarter-million people were sickened by salmonella after consuming Schwan's ice cream. Schwan's wasted no time in denial, blaming or attempts to shift responsibility; instead, they instantly dispatched all home-delivery trucks to every home on their routes to retrieve any delivered ice cream until the source of contamination could be discovered and corrective action taken. They also shut down all ice cream production.

Investigation revealed that a contract trucker had previously hauled contaminated raw eggs before transporting Schwan's ice cream. To solve the problem and minimize chances of recurrence Schwan's bought their own fleet for transporting ingredients, and added a second pasteurization step prior to ice cream packaging.

Today, I still think of Schwan's as a company that stepped up, took responsibility and did the right thing. I'm sure that as with Johnson & Johnson's accountable behavior during the Tylenol crisis from Chapter Three, short-term costs of doing the right thing translated to increased long-term consumer loyalty, brand strength and margins.

OUR MAIN PROMISE

Baruch Spinoza, the seventeenth-century philosopher, believed that "to be what we are, and to become what we are capable of becoming, is the only end in life." I believe that we are all born as a "promise" – some combination of our "calling," values, aims, talents and potential – what I call our "Main Promise." Accountability really begins with discerning that promise – who we intend to be (physically, mentally, emotionally and spiritually,) our purpose or mission, the values we intend to live by, our aims, gifts and talents.

> The realization of the self is only possible if one is productive, if one can give birth to one's own potentialities.
> J.W. von Goethe

Organizations have promising origins as well – their missions, core values, collective talents, goals and potentials to contribute real value. The real "bottom line" that we must keep the main thing – for organizations as well as for individuals — is the degree to which we are living up to that main promise.

COUNTING WHAT COUNTS

Accountability for "keeping the main thing the main thing" and living up to that promise requires paying attention to what counts, or measuring what matters.

Successfully navigating the *Identity* challenge helps us articulate what matters – including our values and principles, purpose, dreams or vision, goals and standards. Some goals, like percentage of market share, revenue and profitability or efficiency for businesses, have built-in measuring mechanisms – we do or do not achieve a goal, or achieve some quantifiable portion of a desired outcome.

However, to paraphrase Albert Einstein, much of what we can count doesn't count much, and some of the things we can't count matter a great deal. Meeting the *Accountability* challenge requires doing our best to establish quantifiable measures for desired outcomes when we can, and at least knowing indicators, or signs of when we are on or off course, when we can't. If our intent is to "be a great dad" or "be a great mom," for instance, there are probably no better indicators (and fewer requiring more courage) than to ask our kids or spouse how we're doing and to ask for examples.

> *Many of the things you can count, don't count. Many of the things you can't count, really count.*
> Albert Einstein

Questions posed in Chapter Three about how we are living our values, and how we are not, serve as good indicators of whether or not we are living up to our promise. Likewise, how far we are on our way to achieving the projections in our organizational or personal visions is also a good indicator. If we aspire to have an excellent organizational culture, high levels of engagement and low turnover compared to other organizations, summaries of exit interviews and organizational climate surveys are all useful to find the degree to which we are living up to those aspirations.

Integrity implies "wholeness;" we will not be whole persons or organizations and the best that we can be by paying attention to measures that reflect only part of the picture. Kaplan and Norton[2] made a significant contribution to management practice by promoting "balanced scorecards" to monitor more than just traditional financial measures of business success. They demonstrated how organizations that excelled at strategic execution measured more than traditional backward-looking, or *lagging,* economic measures of success; they also measured things like customer experiences, internal business processes and learning – real-time *leading* indicators that likely predicted economic success.

Your organization's "balanced scorecard" may look different, but should include means for measuring all the dimensions that matter most. I like five basic measures: *People, Processes, Customers, Stakeholders* and *Profit* (or *Margin* in not-for-profits.)

Order matters; positive *People* and *Process* measures will likely drive desirable *Customer* and *Profit* or *Margin* results – unmotivated people and poor processes will contribute to dissatisfied customers, which will in turn reduce profits or margins. In this respect *People, Process* and *Customer*

> The most serious mistakes are not being made as a result of wrong answers. The truly dangerous thing is asking the wrong question.
>
> Peter Drucker

measures are "leading indicators" because they will likely drive *Profit* or *Margin* measures, the "lagging indicators."

At a personal level, a "balanced scorecard" that reflects the whole picture would help us count what counts not only as "humans doing" but also as "humans being" – physically, mentally, emotionally and spiritually. We might be "successful" by measures of what counts as humans doing – position and possessions, but fall short of the best that we can be across all dimensions of our lives.

We can have leading and lagging indicators within each main dimension of our "scorecard." In an organizational context, dissatisfaction with supervision or promotional opportunities in the *People* dimension would likely be leading indicators contributing to a lagging indicator of unsatisfactory turnover.

For the *Process* dimension, significant waste and re-work in a particular area would be a leading indicator of overall lower process quality or efficiency – a lagging indicator. In a personal context, many months without time for reflection or renewal may result in a decline of our overall quality of life; increasing percentages of declined invitations and unreturned calls or e-mails may be leading indi-

> *Far better an approximate answer to the right question, than the exact answer to the wrong question.*
> John Tukey

cators that quality time for relationships is not what we hoped it would be, or perhaps that we are not living our value of making time for friends. Personally and organizationally, we need leading indicators so we can avoid unpleasant surprises and have opportunities for "mid-course adjustments."

There is so much happening at such a fast pace in most

of our lives that sometimes it's very difficult to give attention to what matters most; everything blurs together and we find ourselves in mainly a reactive mode responding to the "tyranny of the urgent" versus attending to what's truly important. To employ an overworked but useful analogy, more of us could learn from jet pilots who, while remaining aware on some level of many indicators, gauges and alarms, make sure they pay scrupulous attention to the few that matter most: "ADI" (attitude dimension indicator), "HDI" (horizontal dimension indicator), altitude and air speed. What "jet cockpit gauges" should you be paying the most attention to that would help you focus on what matters most?

> *Make the most of yourself, for that is all there is of you.*
> Ralph Waldo Emerson

As a "human doing" — work and professional self:

What are your critical indicators — "jet cockpit gauges" (four or five max) to monitor the degree that you're on course?

How will you monitor these critical indicators?

As a "human being" — physical, mental, emotional and spiritual:

What are your critical indicators — "jet cockpit

gauges" to monitor on a regular basis to know the degree that you're are on course?

How will you monitor these critical indicators?

What do you consider to be the main "scorecard" components (four or five max,) or indicators, for monitoring your organization's performance and health? How are each of the indicators reading, and what do those measures reflect?

ACCOUNTABILITY AND STEWARDSHIP

We commonly think of stewardship as a caretaking role for resources or affairs entrusted to us. It is hard today for anyone in organizations to escape stewardship of financial and physical resources that contribute directly and visibly to the traditional "bottom line," especially those that we have direct responsibility for. Integrity means "wholeness," however; if we have the "whole picture" in mind, accountability requires adopting a broader perspective on our stewardship role.

> *There is only one real failure in life that is possible, and that is, not to be true to the best one knows.*
> Frederic William Farrar

At least one level removed from the physical and financial resources that we typically steward are the less tangible dimensions of human capital– mental, emotional and spiritual, including our own. To paraphrase the Christian apostle Paul, not fully utilizing and developing talents – ours or others', is like "keeping a light under a bushel basket" instead of using it to light the way. Meeting this week's or this quarter's target for financial results, but at the expense of investments in human capital or in ways that exhaust the human spirit, does little for engagement or sustainable results.

In Chapter Three we considered how much of leadership consists of using a larger lens than others use – seeing a "bigger picture." In our role as stewards, seeing things through a larger lens sensitizes us to otherwise unseen, unexamined consequences of our actions. Understanding our larger spheres of influence helps us evaluate the consequences of our decisions and actions on people and resources outside our immediate realm.

> *We ought to think that we are one of the leaves of a tree, and the tree is all humanity. We cannot live without the others, without the tree.*
> Pablo Casals

If in the interest of economy we switch from a local to an overseas supplier, what will the likely impact be in these multiple spheres of influence? How might the loss of revenue in our immediate community affect employment, resources for infrastructure and quality-of-life? What are the working conditions, and what is the environmental record of the overseas supplier? What are the second, third and fourth-order effects of yet another big-box retailer on the edge of our town or in its introduction to the village of a developing nation?

To meet the *Accountability* challenge in our role as stewards we need to adopt not only wider lenses but multiple lenses – assessing the impact beyond just financial ones and the impact of our choices on multiple stakeholders at multiple levels.

"Triple Bottom Line" reporting emerged in the 1990s

as a way to assess sustainability and broaden awareness of organizations' "people, planet and profit" impact. Considering the physical, mental, emotional and spiritual impact of our decisions and actions equips us with an even "higher resolution lens" for evaluating our choices. We need to also utilize longer-range lenses to examine the impact of our decisions and actions, over different time periods and for multiple generations.

No snowflake in an avalanche ever feels responsible.
George Burns

Indigenous cultures that exercised "seventh generation thinking" were more advanced than ours in this respect, considering the consequences of their actions for the seventh generation that followed them. Accountability in its broadest sense will require that institutions and leaders engage in more seventh generational thinking.

To be responsible stewards, most of us need to acquaint ourselves more with the histories and stories of objects and services that we purchase. Not long ago many of us learned for the first time that much of the world's diamond supply has been mined under abhorrent working conditions, including child labor. Even more recently we became alarmed upon discovering the high lead content of toys manufactured in China – lead that not only endangered the health of our children but undoubtedly the health of workers assembling the toys. One need only enter "ethical consumer reports" in an Internet search tool to get a good start learning the stories and "sustainability grades" for many common corporations and brands.

Navigating the *Accountability* challenge and stewardship require broad mindfulness and due diligence – of our actions and their likely second, third, fourth-tier and beyond conse-quences. Not intending adverse consequences or not seeing them does not make us less accountable for them.

In what ways might you exercise better stewardship of resources entrusted to your care, including your own?

Physical, including monetary:

Mental:

Emotional:

Spiritual:

In what ways might your organization exercise better stewardship of these resources?

Physical, including monetary:

Mental:

Emotional:

Spiritual:

What are some actions you can take to learn more about the "stories" or "upstream histories" of materials, products or services that you acquire?

What might you do to extend your awareness of second, third, and fourth-tier consequences of your or your organization's decisions and actions?

ACCOUNTABILITY – KEY POINTS

At a basic level, meeting the *Accountability* challenge so we can live up to our promise means keeping our promises – whether they are promises we make just to ourselves, commitments to others or organizational goals. To deliver on our promises requires keeping track of the promises that we make and not over-promising or under-delivering. If we need to revisit or break a promise, as a check on our priorities and to avoid over-promising in the future, it is important to be honest with ourselves about why.

We all come into this world as a "promise" – potential born of our unique character, gifts and talents, and shaped by our sense of purpose, values and aims; our ultimate accountability is to live up to that "Main Promise." Similarly, at the core of an organization's identity is its "Main Promise" – reflected by its mission, vision, values and brand; again "the main thing is to keep that main thing the main thing."

> *The vast possibilities of our great future will become realities only if we make ourselves responsible for those realities.*
> Gifford Pinchot

What gets measured gets attention; if something matters, we need to measure it somehow. In an organizational setting "the bottom line" may be about profit or margin, but if all of our measures are financial indicators we are likely fixated on the "score" at the expense of playing the "game" the way it needs to be played – and it's likely that even our financial bottom line will deteriorate over time. Taking the whole picture into account, organizations need to monitor "leading indicators" like *People, Process* and *Customer* measures in addition to financial measures. Showing up as *whole leaders* requires paying attention to all of who we and others are: physically, mentally, emotionally and spiritually.

Accountability means taking responsibility – seeing problems, owning them, solving them and executing solutions – <u>not</u> seeking to shift blame, escape responsibility or just look good. Accountability also requires that we be good stewards – of our own resources and those entrusted to us. Especially today we need to exercise conscientious stewardship of people as resources; it is their passion, engagement, creativity and capacity that will carry the day competitively in a rapidly changing, increasingly complex global marketplace.

True leadership, sustainability and integrity require a "long view." The famed strategist Miyamoto Musashi[3] advised us to "see distant things as they are close and close things as they are distant." Effective stewardship requires that ability to see the distant effect of our decisions and actions today – where "distance" may be measured in many miles or many generations.

I hope that some of the "whys" and "hows" to this point for navigating the *Identity, Authenticity, Alignment* and *Accountability* integrity challenges will enrich your life and help you cultivate organizational cultures that are effective, ethical and engaging. It's unlikely that many organizations or persons set out to not have integrity or to not be effective, ethical and engaging. Yet even knowing much of what's been covered so far, it is more difficult to put it into practice. The next chapter will help you and your organization develop six critical capabilities to navigate the four integrity challenges and transform from business as usual to its best.

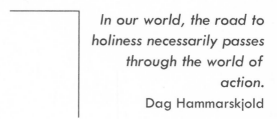

In our world, the road to holiness necessarily passes through the world of action.
Dag Hammarskjold

One can no more navigate the four integrity challenges by just reading about them than to become a good sailor by reading sailing books. We already know that much of what precedes this chapter is important, but knowing and doing are two different things. We know that we should speak up or tell the truth, but we don't; we know about the importance of hearing everyone out, but we don't consistently; we've known for years that our work isn't a good fit, but we don't initiate any changes.

Why do we sometimes know but not act? In many cases we likely fall short because we lack the capability required. No doubt there are more, but for me, six capabilities stand out as critical for navigating the four integrity challenges here: first, *Competence* – the knowledge, skills and abilities required for tasks that we commit to, and two other "Cs" – *Consistency* and *Courage*, plus three "Ds": *Discipline, Discernment,* and *Dialog.*

COMPETENCE

Part of the trust that integrity inspires is that a leader, organization or team has what it takes to accomplish what needs to be done. One of a boat skipper's first tasks before undertaking a voyage is to realistically assess his or her and the crew's capabilities; failing to do so puts the voyage as well as everyone's lives at risk.

In the same vein, leaders must realistically assess their own capabilities and help others do the same if they are to fulfill their commitments. Just as important is realistically assessing the nature and difficulty of tasks as well as the conditions in which they will be performed and the time available to complete them. Self-knowledge, part of navigating the *Identity* challenge, is critical here. Also essential is the ability to see things as they are and not as we wish them to be, part of navigating the *Authenticity* challenge.

Integrity includes delivering on the commitments we make, so care must be taken to not promise more than we can deliver. What happens when we determine that the competencies or resources required to meet a commitment are greater than those we possess? Our first responsibility is to be honest with ourselves about the gap, then to make a realistic assessment of whether we can close it sufficiently to meet obligations while remaining true to our values.

"Remaining true to our values" is critical here; "doing whatever it takes" to meet performance requirements does not follow the path of integrity if it means violating other commitments or our core values. For example, a wholesale swap-out of an entire team for another with competencies that are a better fit would certainly be questionable when a professed value is workforce retention or loyalty. If we cannot close a gap between the capabilities that we have and those required to meet commitments, an honorable path is to admit it when we know it, then perhaps negotiate performance requirements or collaborate with others in order to meet them.

A large consulting firm contacted me not long ago because they won a contract requiring strong facilitation of challenging executive-level meetings. There's no doubt in my mind that there were individuals in their firm who could have gotten by facilitating the meeting at a much lower cost than retaining a sub-contractor, but "getting by" didn't square with their values. I was not surprised to discover not long afterward that the same consulting firm was named by the *Ethisphere Institute* as one of the year's most ethical business services firms.

Living up to our promise and potential demands growth; yesterday's answers and solutions will seldom be sufficient for

> *Life's greatest achievement is the continual re-making of yourself so that at last you know how to live.*
> Winfred Rhodes

tomorrow's challenges, and we must constantly be "sharpening our saw" as Stephen Covey reminds us. He asks us to imagine walking through the forest and encountering a woodsman who has been laboring feverishly for hours cutting down trees without ever stopping to sharpen his saw. The results are, of course, getting poorer and poorer, and the process is taking a tremendous toll on the woodsman. When asked why he hasn't sharpened his saw since starting, he replies that there simply hasn't been time.

We learned in Chapter Five that *Accountability* requires paying attention to what matters. Stephen Covey[1] classifies things that matter and that are also urgent as "Quadrant 1." He classifies "Quandrant 2" matters as things that are important but not urgent, and therefore that require more conscious and disciplined effort. Most "saw sharpening," or self-development tasks fall

> *An effective human being is a whole greater than the sum of its parts.*
> Ida P. Rolf

into this quadrant, which Covey dubs the "quadrant of personal leadership." (Covey's "Quadrant 3" consists of things that are urgent but relatively unimportant, and "Quadrant 4" is filled with activities that mainly waste our time.)

Whole leadership requires growth in all dimensions of who we are. Intellectual giants who are "midgets" emotionally or morally will not only fall short of their potential, but may very well do harm; for evidence we have only to remember the Wall Street "whiz kids" who brought down our economy. The investment bankers and traders populating the likes of Lehman Brothers and Goldman Sachs were among the best and brightest intellectually among their MBA graduating class. What led to Lehman Brothers' demise and Goldman Sachs' troubles was not lack of intellectual capacity, but falling short in other dimensions of their development.

We need to not only keep up with the times in terms of <u>what</u> we know, but also continue cultivating our mental capacities and getting better at learning how to learn. Our physical health and capacity is naturally connected to our mental, emotional and spiritual well-being; eventually our ability to process what is going on conceptually or

> *You are all things. Denying, rejecting, judging or hiding from any aspect of your total being creates pain and results in a lack of wholeness.*
>
> Joy Page

emotionally declines when we are exhausted, not exercising or abusing our physical health in other ways. For many of us, in the Western industrialized world especially, emotional and spiritual development are likely even deeper in "Quadrant 2" than our mental and physical development – critically important, but often overlooked because they may seem to be the least urgent or pressing.

The effects of not knowing an answer to a technical question at work or to a critical question in a board meeting may be more readily apparent and immediate – or so we think – than missing emotional cues in a meeting or relationship. Failure in either regard, however, will jeopardize results. Similarly, most of us will likely connect poor sleeping or eating habits with poor results more readily than knowing the effects of neglecting our spiritual or moral development.

A balanced development plan that addresses mental, physical, emotional and spiritual capacities will stimulate our growth as whole leaders and as whole organizations. A solid foundation for any development plan includes base measures of some sort for where we are compared to where we could be. We have become quite sophisticated measuring physical health and capacities – heart and lung capacity, strength and coordination, visual and hearing acuity, ability to meet physical job requirements, genetic predisposition to certain diseases, etc. We have also become very precise (but some would argue perhaps not very accurate) when it comes to measuring intelligence and mental capacity – traditional IQ tests, measures of mathematical, verbal and spatial reasoning, plus the many measures and tests devised to assess the extent to which workers and professionals have a command of the knowledge required for their trade.

> The time has come to openly acknowledge the contribution of moral intelligence to effective leadership and sustainability.
>
> Doug Lennick and Fred Kiel

Thanks to Daniel Goleman[2] and his predecessors John D. Mayer and Peter Salovey, we have come to understand that Emotional Intelligence, or "EQ," is different than traditional IQ, and is also a significant contributor to leadership effectiveness. By 1997 there were sixty separate instruments available that purportedly measured emotional intelligence. More recently Doug Lennick and Fred Kiel[3] described the characteristics of moral intelligence in a book by that title, which includes a Moral Competency Inventory.

Self-reports alone of personal characteristics and capabilities have limitations; you may want to explore available objective measures and seek others' input as you answer the following questions:

What might your development plan include for things you want to learn more about or for <u>mental</u> capacities that you want to develop?

What should likely be in your <u>physical</u> development plan — health, strength, endurance, physical skills . . .?

What "<u>emotional</u> intelligence" (including self-awareness, self-control, emotional awareness and relationship management) and "moral intelligence" (including integrity, responsibility, compassion and forgiveness) development goals do you have? How might you achieve those goals?

Do you have any spiritual or moral development goals — and how might you work on those?

Competency appraisals and balanced development plans are critical for teams and organizations as well. To achieve their aims and fulfill their commitments they will benefit from a realistic sense of what capabilities they possess and their relative strength, along with what it would take to close any gaps.

As with individuals, if teams and organizations are to live up to their whole promise, they need to consider not only physical and mental capacities, but emotional, spiritual and moral intelligences as well. Do they have the resources and capabilities to manage relationships, nurture a sense of meaning and significance, and consistently act ethically? We are more accustomed to auditing our organizations' physical and mental capabilities than their emotional and moral capacities; if we are in touch with reality and are honest with ourselves, however, we probably realize that the biggest and longest-term threats to the health and success of our organizations will come from insufficient emotional, spiritual and moral reserves.

Does your organization have a realistic sense of its strengths and of its capabilities that need development?

If you crafted a development plan for your organization, what would that look like?
Physical capacity and health:

Mental capacity and knowledge:

"Emotional intelligence:"

"Moral intelligence:"

Spiritual development:

DISCIPLINE

"Discipline" and "disciple" share the same Latin root: discipulus, meaning "follower" or "learner." We exercise discipline when we faithfully follow a path, set of principles or values to achieve goals, and when we follow a regimen that teaches or guides us in ways that develop our capacities. We are disciplined when we consistently make decisions and choose to behave in ways that are aligned with our

> *We are what we repeatedly do. Excellence, then, is not an act, but a habit.*
> Aristotle

values   and aims – especially when distractions and temptations make that difficult, and when we consistently apply our energies in ways that develop our capacities and more wholesome habits. Making progress with our development plans from the last section – living up to those promises, will require above all discipline – choosing to develop habits and apply ourselves in ways that do not come naturally.

> *The law of the harvest is to reap more than you sow. Sow an act, and you reap a habit; sow a habit, and you reap a character; sow a character and you reap a destiny.*
> G. D. Boardman

Discipline is fed by, and in turn feeds, all four dimensions of the leadership and organizational integrity model: *Identity, Authenticity, Alignment* and *Accountability.*

Navigating the *Identity* challenge arms us with a sufficiently strong sense of purpose and values to bolster the motivation, as well as the discipline required to make hard decisions or to change counterproductive behaviors. It also builds sufficient self-awareness to know where there are gaps in required capabilities and what "shadows" may interfere with the necessary discipline to do what's needed; "fore-warned is fore-armed." For example if I know that I have a tendency for wanting to please people and avoid conflict, I can be extra vigilant about standing my ground and working on my assertiveness when important principles are at stake.

Navigating the *Authenticity* challenge and realizing that our actions are out of tune with our values can stimulate the discipline required for acting to close those gaps. Navigating the *Authenticity* challenge also nurtures the discipline required to listen for new information and for divergent points of view so we can see things as they are versus how we wish them to be.

Navigating the *Alignment* challenge stimulates the discipline needed for being faithful to core ideology and simultaneously questioning what we need to change so we can be more in tune with the times and market demands.

Navigating the *Accountability* challenge stimulates the discipline that we need for measuring what matters in some way and for devoting time and resources to those things that matter most.

Discipline is an act of will that requires consciously choosing to replace one set of reactions or habits with new behaviors; whenever relapse threatens, we need to consciously behave differently than before.

There are four primary levers that can help organizations and individuals exercise that type of will: First, we need reminders of our purpose, vision, aims and values – those things we are drawn to and that remind us why it is important to do things differently.

Secondly, we need to remind ourselves of the consequences if we are not able to change habits or behaviors and are not able to achieve our aims. Clear-Way Minnesota,® an organization devoted to eliminating the health hazards of tobacco, did a particularly effective job of this through its public service ads. In one, after viewing clips of a father preparing to walk his daughter down the aisle on her wedding,

> *Thoughts lead on to purposes; purposes go forth in action; actions form habits; habits decide character; and character fixes our destiny.*
> Tryon Edwards

we witness the father hooked up to a respirator in a hospital bed and dying of cancer. The closing message is: "If you aren't planning to quit smoking, what are you planning?"

Some kind of code, regimen, protocol or set of rules to follow is a third way to strengthen discipline so we can achieve the ends we seek. After following protocols or rules for behavior that may seem foreign or difficult at first, they eventually become second-nature and get woven into new and better habitual behavior; sleeping and arising at regular times, showering or bathing, brushing our teeth and flossing, exercising and grooming are familiar personal examples.

One of the oldest, most highly regarded collection of "rules" in the Western World is "The Rule of Saint Benedict[4]." Written approximately fifteen hundred years ago, it not only provided guidelines for monks to live in community and for *ora et labora* (prayer and work) but also a set of leadership, community-building and right-living principles still relevant today.

Coaching and support is a fourth tool for cultivating

discipline. Adopting and following any regimen, set of principles or "rules" will likely be more successful with support from others; running or exercise buddies, most "12-step" programs and coaching are examples. Sometimes the support needed for following a discipline or changing behaviors can take the form of simple agreements among friends so we can be reminded if we slip back to old behaviors.

I have to admit that I have been a little anxious writing about discipline, since I am not very disciplined myself in some arenas. I am more disciplined about a daily exercise routine than I am about finances, for example, and am more disciplined about delivering what I commit to current clients than the marketing it takes to acquire new ones. That may be a good starting point – simply noting and owning those arenas in our lives that would benefit from more discipline.

What are some areas of your life or work that you think would benefit from more discipline?

What are the possibilities — for you and for others — if you were to replace one set of behaviors or habits in those areas with others? What could you do . . . achieve . . . be?

What are the likely consequences — for you and others — if you are not able to introduce more discipline and different behaviors in those arenas?

For each of those arenas where you would like to introduce more discipline, what is a regimen, routine or set of "rules" that would help shape the behaviors and change you desire?

Who, or what support, would be helpful for you to establish the discipline and change your behaviors as needed in those arenas?

In your organization or team:
Where could your team / organization use more discipline, and how will that help?

What are some steps you and others might take, or habits / "rules" you might adopt to establish needed discipline and help shape desired behaviors?

What support, help or resources might help your team / organization develop needed discipline?

CONSISTENCY

Let's talk about consistency next since it is a close cousin of discipline. We develop new and better habits or patterns of behaving if we consistently apply discipline and consistently choose new behaviors over old ones. I heard that it takes about 10,000 repetitions for a new skill or behavior to become automatic and part of who we are. That is why countless repetitions and drills are important for martial arts training and most sports; we want the reactions and behavior to become second nature and automatic without having to think about them.

Thousands of repetitions and consistency are important not only to help us truly integrate new behaviors and habits, but to help others' perceptions catch up with who we are becoming. I shared in Chapter Two that "excitability" is part of my personality profile. A "dark side" of that temperament is that unless I train, or discipline, myself to behave differently I may overreact, or react without thinking to someone's behavior or comment. No doubt there are still folks who see me as overly excitable despite my efforts to behave differently. Perhaps they need to experience my new behavior ten thousand times for their perceptions to catch up with who I am becoming. If I'm not consistent, and I slip up once in a while, others' perceptions may go back to square one.

> *The shortest and surest way to live with honor in the world is to be in reality with what would appear to be; and if we observe we will find that all human virtues increase and strengthen themselves by the practice and experience of them.*
> Socrates

Consistency, like the congruency in our Chapter Four "tapestries of intention," is critical for trust. To trust that behavior is genuine and that we can count on it, we generally need to experience consistent behavior on multiple occasions and circumstances over a long period. A person might behave consistently in certain settings, but if we witness different behavior on other occasions,

> *Without consistency there is no moral strength.*
> John Owen

things just "don't add up." We might witness a loving, considerate and respectful parent in a home setting become an autocratic, tyrannical and inconsiderate supervisor in a work setting. Which is real? Not long ago, the nation witnessed the fall of a prominent state governor who had earned a reputation as a hard-lined, ruthless, law-and-order district attorney when it turned out that over a number of years he had been the customer of high-priced call-girl services.

When someone says or does things differently in one setting than in others, we are confused about what to believe. Of course when words and deeds are incongruent, we generally believe the deeds and distrust the words (and person); as Emerson said: "Your actions speak so loudly I cannot hear what you are saying!"

Consistency and congruency are also critical for cultures of trust in organizations. In Chapter Two we talked about the importance of designing hiring, pay and training programs to be congruent with an organization's values and strategic aims. Consistently *administering* hiring, pay and training programs is also essential. For example, trust in the integrity of a merit pay program is eroded when the standards for what constitutes "excellent" performance in one organizational unit are different than in another. Likewise, if training is treated as an essential investment by some but an optional expense by others in the same organization, trust in the integrity of the organization and in its development programs will erode.

> No one man can, for any considerable time, wear one face to himself, and another to the multitude, without finally getting bewildered as to which is the true one.
>
> Nathaniel Hawthorne

Behavior, especially of the founders and senior executives, needs to be consistent and congruent with espoused values and aims to generate believability and trust. One of the greatest contributors to confusion and distrust in organizations that I encounter is when an executive communicates inconsistently at different times or with different audiences; which is true and what should we believe? Another big contributor is when messages or behavior are inconsistent across an executive group or board. Boards and executive groups need to accommodate different perspectives and work through divergent points of view on their own, then act and communicate consistently with the outside.

In a workshop with all managers and supervisors of a health-care system, inconsistency accounted for two primary barriers to organizational integrity that they identified. One was inconsistency between standards of care for hospital admissions during the day and those for night admissions. The other – which frankly I have encountered a great deal in healthcare settings – was shabby treatment and disrespect of non-doctors by a few of the doctors, and inconsistency around disciplining those behaviors.

There must be consistency in direction.

W. Edwards Deming

To this health system's credit, and as a testament to the integrity and truth-telling culture it already had, those inconsistencies were reported by a table of nurses to the entire group of over one hundred administrators, including the health system's CEO and the Chief Medical officer – a doctor.

After a few moments of "pregnant silence," I witnessed part of what contributed to the system's existing truth-telling culture and integrity. First the Chief Medical officer stood up and announced that moving forward he would take personal responsibility to assure consistently respectful treatment of staff by all doctors, and he invited all present to confidentially report any future disrespectful encounters to him directly (which was greeted by applause.) After more discussion, the CEO announced a task force to examine inconsistencies around quality of care for day versus night admissions and to recommend an action plan.

In Chapter Four we talked about the importance of balance in meeting the *Alignment* challenge, including the importance of balancing stability with adaptability. While consistency is important, there are times when integrity may call more for adaptability than consistency, like when we need to adjust our response for specific circumstances.

What may look like inconsistent or preferential treatment, for example, may in fact demonstrate more fairness and compassion than would equal treatment. I know there are appropriate precautions to take around favoritism and discrimination, but if motives have integrity, fair and compassionate treatment might mean granting some staff members greater schedule flexibility than others. In circumstances like these we need to clearly communicate our intentions, what we are doing and why. For example if schedule flexibility is granted to some employees more than others, a manager should find appropriate opportunities to openly communicate the decisions about schedule flexibility, why they were made, the values or principle that decisions were based on and as much as possible about what criteria or standards were applied. Then of course, the manager needs to be "consistently inconsistent" applying those criteria or standards in the future.

> *A foolish consistency is the hobgoblin of little minds.*
> Ralph Waldo Emerson

> *There are those who would misteach us that to stick in a rut is consistency- and a virtue; and that to climb out of the rut is inconsistency- and a vice.*
> Mark Twain

Another context where meeting the *Alignment* challenge may call for relaxing consistency is altering traditions in response to changes in technology or other external variables. For example, it may be time to replace traditional in-person gatherings with "virtual meetings" as the quality of the required technology increases and its cost decreases. In most business settings over the last few years we've witnessed relaxed consistency enforcing dress codes as those standards have evolved. Consistency and tradition can be important, but there comes a time when we need to question the utility of some consistencies.

Where in your life or work do you think you might be inconsistent? How do you think that affects your life, work or relationships? (This is for sure a question where you will want to get some candid input from a trusted friend or associate.)

What might you do to show up more consistently?

Where do you see inconsistencies in your organization or at work that you think are affecting performance or trust? What might you do to bring that to others' attention and help reduce inconsistencies?

Can you think of any ways — in life or at work — that perhaps you should be <u>less</u> consistent, or where you might question whether some things you have always done a certain way should change?

DISCERNMENT AND DIALOG

Let's take these two "Ds" together since they serve a common purpose: to determine what is right – which is the right view, the right decision or the right course of action. *Discernment* can be an individual or a group process; in a relationship or group we have the added benefit of *dialog* to enlarge the arena of perspectives, knowledge or options.

Sometimes discernment needs to be an individual process if the need to act is urgent or if a decision is personal – as in *discerning* a vocation. Otherwise as a rule we are better off taking advantage of numbers and multiple perspectives to make the best deci-

Truth, when not sought after, rarely comes to light.

Oliver Wendell Holmes

sions. We may think there is more urgency to decide or act than there really is, or that a decision is ours alone to make – and end up taking even more time down the road to undo a solo decision or action.

Discernment involves gathering and paying attention to whatever facts, data, perceptions or other input we can to help us decide or make sense of a situation; the more diverse the input, the better. Paying attention to only factual data and neglecting emotions, hunches or how we and others feel, or paying attention to just one source of input (to one party vs. others, or to just audio and not visual cues) leaves us playing with a "partial deck."

We need to do something with whatever data, facts, hunches, feelings or input that we have – usually come to a conclusion, make a decision or take action. There is a "doing something before we do something" phase, however, that usually counts the most. It may simply be pausing; a "pause that refreshes" is often sufficient to help us make better sense of what we've heard or what we're feeling so we can respond appropriately. As someone said, if we react too quickly or in anger, we "may end up making the best speech we will ever regret."

Discernment is essentially a careful, responsible assessment and decision-making process that begins with discriminating choices about what observations and input we attend to. Too often we attend most to what we are already familiar with or think we know. Unfortunately, we then end up confirming conclusions that we were already predisposed to, and the real value of the exercise is lost.

The most valuable observations and input will be those that challenge our existing perceptions and opinions so that we have the widest array of perspectives to use when deciding what to do. We need to determine what senses, information or information sources to trust. Is there anything different about this situation or context that could alter reliability? *Can I trust this data or person? Can I trust my senses here? Once again, self awareness is critical: Where or with whom am I overly trusting or distrusting? Given my character (as in Myers-Briggs preferences for intuition and hunches vs. facts and figures,) might I be missing something here? Might I want to believe something enough that I am blind to disconfirming information?*

Having data, observations and input – and hopefully sufficient amounts from diverse perspectives, we need to make sense of it all. *What does what we're seeing and hearing mean? Are there alternate explanations or plausible interpretations?* As a demonstration of how other perspectives often help, an associate used

> Not the truth of which one supposes himself possessed, but the effort he has made to arrive at the truth, makes the worth of the man. For not by the possession, but by the investigation, of truth are his powers expanded.
> Gotthold Ephraim Lessing

to offer me this advice when I was on the verge of jumping to a conclusion about someone's statement or behavior: "Now ask yourself – what are some reasons why a normal, rational person might say or do that?" Merely pausing sufficiently to ask myself that question and generate possible explanations beyond those that I assumed were true have led to better conclusions and outcomes over time.

Discernment is required to think through the second, third, fourth-order and beyond consequences of our decisions and actions. *If I do this, then what will possibly or likely happen? What will possibly or likely happen after that? Who will be affected, and in what ways? Are there longer term consequences, or stakeholders who may be affected that have not been taken into account?*

> Healing of the world's woes will not come through this or that social or political theory; not through violent changes in government, but in the still small voice that speaks to the conscience and the heart.
>
> Arthur J. Moore

Often integrity and living up to the best we are capable of requires discerning which of two or more "rights" is the best path, or which sets of potentially negative consequences should most be avoided. These situations in particular call for care to collect and consider multiple, diverse perspectives, and to take time for careful thought and deliberation about the best course of action.

Sometimes retreating from usual surroundings, others' opinions or distractions improves discernment. Sigurd Olson, protector, benefactor and documentarian of the wilderness Boundary Waters Canoe Area in Minnesota referred to his cabin in the woods and retreat from distractions as his "listening point." We can all use such a listening point; teams as well benefit by "retreating" from familiar surroundings to have different kinds of conversations. (Although I always believed that those experiences, when done well, should be called "advances" instead of "retreats"!)

My "listening point" is just about any sunset – especially over water where something about the light, quiet and setting make for a different way to reflect on the day, particular events, decisions to make, problems to solve or actions to plan. I also find that physical work, especially outdoors, engages me in a different way than other routines and helps generate insights that I would not otherwise have had. Of course my favorite "listening point" is usually the cockpit of our sailboat, especially standing watch in only moonlight on a starry night or at sunset.

> *Only in quiet waters things mirror themselves undistorted. Only in a quiet mind is adequate perception of the world.*
> Everett W. Lord

There are times requiring discernment where it is impossible to retreat to our physical "listening points;" then sometimes just breathing or a form of meditation or prayer might help. (Which for many provide an even more powerful boost when adopted as a regular discipline.)

How might you improve your own personal capability for discernment?

When and how might you make more effective use of pausing ("the pause that refreshes") to improve the quality of your conclusions or responses?

Are there different or additional perspectives or sources of data and input that might improve the quality of your discernment efforts?

If you have a "listening point," how might you make more or better use of it? If you don't have one, or could use a better one, where or what might that be?

When you cannot access a physical listening point, how might you incorporate breathing or some form of meditation or prayer to help with discernment?

Dialog is essentially a "learning conversation" that enhances a group's discernment capabilities – a group of two or of thousands. Learning conversations are very different from what many of us are accustomed to. Most of us, in business settings especially, are used to presentations with a strong point of view or to variations on debates and discussions – where the goal is usually to convince someone of something or for our ideas to prevail.

> *Do not search for truth. Just stop having opinions.*
> Seng - Ts'an

If we already have an answer, solution or course of action in mind, it is likely well thought through and very rational, and we've become pretty attached to it – so attached that it is quite difficult, if not impossible, to imagine any other way of seeing things.

There are four necessary conditions for effective dialog: We need to first slow down and not be in a rush for an answer, <u>the</u> answer or a solution. Second, we need to adopt an air of curiosity or inquisitiveness. We then need to state and examine our assumptions – things that we believe to be true or assume to be the case, and help others examine theirs. And, most importantly, we need to engage in conversation with open minds, a willingness to change them and the intent to learn.

Believe those who are seeking the truth; doubt those who have found it.

Andre Gide

Questions are the "coin of the realm" for effective dialog – but different kinds of questions than are often asked. Many times, in heated discussions especially, we hear questions intended to make a statement, trip someone up or gain an advantage. In contrast, true dialog makes use of questions that invite others to share more about their points of view and to learn something new. Questions are asked out of genuine curiosity to learn what others are seeing, assuming or thinking, and why.

Questions asked out of genuine curiosity or in a manner that generates more possibilities stimulate dialog: *"I wonder what they may be seeing that we are not? . . . I wonder if these assumptions are true? . . . I wonder what would be possible if this were not the case? . . . I wonder what would happen if . . . ?"*

Dialog requires real listening, not pseudo-listening – when we send signals that we're listening but are in fact biding our time to state our own opinion or collecting evidence to prove others wrong.

When the famous WWII General Douglas MacArthur was asked about the secret to his success he said: "Three things: Listen to the other person's story, listen to the other person's <u>whole</u> story, and listen to the other person's whole story <u>first</u>." I have witnessed truly remarkable breakthroughs and the resolution of many deadlocks when parties were able to simply adopt the discipline of real listening.

It seems comforting to some when I assure them that after really listening there will be adequate time and opportunity to disagree with what they've heard should they choose to and to state their own opinions. What's funny is that when parties in an initially heated exchange start really listening, their views often converge or they come up with a path forward that none had previously thought of. Even when that doesn't happen, relationships almost always improve and the ground is more fertile for future productive exchanges.

What occasions or situations do you see or participate in that would benefit from better dialog?

What will you do to stimulate and reinforce real listening and dialog in those situations?

COURAGE

Integrity and courage are pretty much inseparable; where we see one, we will generally see the other. Without integrity, much of what passes for courage might be mainly adrenaline, and integrity without courage resembles the proverbial "light under a bushel basket" – untested, and providing no illumination where it's needed most. Courage is required to successfully navigate all of the integrity challenges.

IDENTITY AND COURAGE

It can take a lot of courage to own who we are, especially when who we are and what we value are contrary to the norm or to what pays. It takes even more courage to be who we are and to act on our values in the face of opposition, uncertainty about the outcomes, rejection or adverse economic consequences. Vincent van Gogh was rejected by the art critics of his day and never sold one of his works while he was alive, yet he persisted painting what he saw in his own style. Today he is one of history's most revered artists and none of his works can be purchased for less than a million dollars; the courage to be who we are and live what we believe to be true sometimes extracts a short-term price, but can eventually deliver great value.

> *With courage you will dare to take risks, have the strength to be compassionate, and the wisdom to be humble. Courage is the foundation of integrity.*
> Keshavan Nair

It took courage when Howard Schultz, Starbucks' founder, wrote an open letter to the Starbucks Board stating that Starbucks was losing its way as offerings diversified away from high quality coffee experiences. It takes courage when an assisted living facility remains true to its mission of consistently "providing environments that nurture self-worth, hope and dignity" in the face of rising costs and declines in reimbursement rates.

In what ways do you display the courage of owning who you are and standing up for what you believe?

How / when might you summon the courage to do that even more?

What are ways that your organization displays the courage to "keep its main thing the main thing" and consistently live its values even at a cost? What are ways that it might display even more of that kind of courage?

AUTHENTICITY AND COURAGE

It takes courage to tell the truth, including to ourselves – about a failing relationship, an unworkable business plan, a job that is not a good fit or things that just aren't true but we wish were so.

Because it can be difficult to face some truths alone, it's a blessing when friends or associates have the courage to help us see them, and when we have the courage to do the same for others or for our organizations.

Max DePree stated "a leader's first responsibility is to face reality." If we are a leader, we first need to see and have the courage to face unpleasant realities ourselves, then we need to articulate them and mobilize others for action. It takes courage to tell the truth as we see it, especially when voicing contrary opinions in meetings or disagreeing with the boss.

> *Have the courage to say no. Have the courage to face the truth. Do the right thing because it is right. Theses are the magic keys to living your life with integrity.*
> W. Clement Stone

Associates and clients tell me that perhaps the most common breakdown of integrity and courage in organizations is reluctance to speak up, voice contrary opinions or disagree with others out of fear of reprisal. Unfortunately, sometimes those fears are well founded and there is a price to pay. The alternative costs, however, can be higher in the long-term.

How many people lose a bit of their souls each day by not mustering the courage to speak their truth, and over time lose any capability to stand up for what they believe is right? As the saying goes: "A hero dies only once, but those who lack courage die a thousand deaths."

Most people stumble over the truth, but they manage to pick themselves up and go on anyway.

Wintston Churchill

The costs for organizations that stifle truth-telling and for their stakeholders are often higher, as evinced by countless examples like the Enron and WorldCom fiascoes or the Countrywide Financial and Bear Stearns' meltdowns. The space shuttle *Challenger* would likely not have blown up in 1986, killing all seven astronauts, had those in the Morton Thiokol / NASA chain of command made their voices heard about faulty O-ring seals.

Where or how might you speak out more about what you see, hear or believe for the sake of your or your organization's integrity or for those you serve?

What are ways that your organization might cultivate and reinforce more of the courage required to speak up or speak out when that is difficult?

ALIGNMENT AND COURAGE

We need the courage not only to speak our own convictions, but also to have our convictions challenged, truly listen to those with contrary opinions and admit that we don't have a lock on the truth. Discernment requires the courage to let go of familiar "truths" so we can really explore alternative views. Much of what doesn't seem to be working in organizations and communities these days (think "blue" and "red" states or congressional deadlocks) is a lot of talking past one another. We need to get better at letting go of the truths that we think we know and seeking a "middle way" or creative solution to move things forward without alienation or disengagement. Healing the wounds and closing the gaps that divide us require courage to speak our minds and hearts, courage to help others do the same and courage to engage in true dialog so we can mine our differences for the best results.

> *One isn't necessarily born with courage, but one is born with potential. Without courage, we cannot practice any other virtue with consistency. We can't be kind, true, merciful, generous or honest.*
> Maya Angelou

Where might having the courage to really listen to alternative points of view and to engage in real dialog reduce alienation, build community and facilitate progress?

Courage is often also required to heal wounds or divides in our personal or work lives. It is one thing to recognize, for example, that our work or where we work is at odds with who we are and what we value; it usually takes more courage to act on that awareness. We need to face questions like: "What about the mortgage?" "What about retirement?" What will friends and family members think?" "Am I willing to sacrifice the trappings of conventional success?"

We probably all have some friends and acquaintances who have, and some who haven't yet, mustered the courage to actually take the first steps for creating more alignment between who they are and what they do.

Yes, taking those steps means greater uncertainty and likely short-term costs; long-term, however, the upsides for them, their loved ones and often their employer are likely significantly greater.

I have often thought morality may consist solely in the courage of making a choice.
Leon Blum

What courageous steps can you take now that will create more alignment between who you are and what you are doing or who you are doing it with?

ACCOUNTABILITY AND COURAGE

Keeping our promises and delivering on our commitments often require courage. Being the best that we can be requires the courage to set, and more importantly, to achieve challenging objectives and standards. We must have the courage to admit when, how and why we fall short ourselves, and to confront others who may not be measuring up.

> *You gain strength, courage, and confidence by every experience in which you really stop to look fear in the face. You must do the thing which you think you cannot do.*
> Eleanor Roosevelt

Accountability means having the courage and discipline to pay attention to what matters and to take action when we are off course. For example it takes courage for faculty members to speak out because they believe that attention paid to lucrative consulting or research revenue detracts from a university's teaching mission. Accountability for results that add value, especially if unconventional, requires courage to depart from familiar or routine practices, and to make sacrifices for something that is still unknown or unproven.

To be accountable means that we are good stewards, and that we take responsibility for the impact of our decisions and actions on others, however far removed. Acting responsibly on the knowledge of how our decisions and actions affect others can require courage, not to mention considerable creativity and resourcefulness. It takes courage, for example, to switch from a low-cost overseas supplier that engages in unfair labor practices when the balance of global competitors defines accountability more narrowly.

How might you exercise more courage to deliver on your commitments?

How might exercising more courage help you pay closer attention to what matters most or to effects of decisions and actions that have gone unnoticed? What are ways that your organization has demonstrated courage to be truly accountable and a responsible steward? What are ways that it might display even more of that kind of courage?

Winston Churchill told us "courage does not mean the absence of fear, but acting in the face of our fears." How do we develop the capacity for that? How or why does one organization or person muster the courage to do what needs to be done but others do not? How do we find the courage to act in some situations but not in others?

One way to fortify our courage is to remind ourselves and others of what matters most. On a personal level we can focus on our purpose, our values, whom we love and how we want to be remembered. Knowing what we live for can give us strength to live with nearly any <u>how</u>. Organizations too can revitalize their sense of purpose, remind members of their work's significance and impact, and draw upon organizational values or stories for inspiration.

The word "courage" is derived from the French "coeur," and literally means "of the heart." The heart is a muscle; like other muscles we can test and fortify our courage incrementally – exercising it first with matters of smaller significance and building up "strength of heart" for more consequential matters: A person with an unhealthy dependency first finds the courage to forego the dependency one day, then a week, then months, then years. We find the strength to voice unpopular opinions in small meetings with peers, then in meetings with our boss, and eventually in large groups where the stakes are even higher. A business first chooses a supplier more aligned with its core values at a slight inconvenience, then works its way to forming strategic partnerships with more ethical suppliers, even though for the short-term it may mean a competitive disadvantage and a hit in its stock price.

While a true test of courage and integrity is the ability to do what's right on our own, a supportive community – family, friends or co-workers – encourages the heart. We need to find others who support our courageous steps and seek how we can provide such support to others. Leaders and organizations that wish to "en-courage" integrity need to state their values clearly and welcome, even invite, feedback when word and deed seem not to be aligned.

To strengthen courage, how might you connect more with what matters most to you, including your purpose and values?

Are there smaller decisions or opportunities to take risks that will enable more courageous decisions and action?

How might you connect with others and use the strength of community to support your or others' courageous decisions and actions?

What are some strategies you can employ to strengthen courage in your organization?

PARTING WORDS

I completed the manuscript for this book around the time of the real estate market's collapse, the meltdown of financial institutions worldwide, Bernie Madoff's $50 billion Ponzi scheme, the bottom (we hoped) of a forty-five percent drop in the Dow Jones and mounting distrust in our institutions and those who led them. When associates heard that I was going to publish a book on leadership and organizational integrity, the typical response was "What great timing!" Yes – and no. Yes, because we certainly need to re-ground our institutions and notions of leadership around enduring principles and strength of character. We will not get out of these messes and stay out for long without sufficient attention to navigating these four integrity challenges and developing our "3C and 3D" capabilities.

In another way, the timing of this book is nothing special. Attending to these challenges has always been critical – no more today than they were two, ten, twenty or two hundred years ago; we simply lost our way and need to remember the fundamentals for assuring sustainable value while living core values. Another potential downside to this book's timing is that our most recent economic crisis prompted a knee-jerk reaction of "let's get down to brass tacks" and not waste any time on any of the "soft, nice-to-have stuff." I think it was the day I finished my first manuscript draft that I read an article stating that "we're in an economic dip, and the last thing the business world is concerned with is once popular terms like 'emotional intelligence' and 'corporate responsibility.' It is high season for cost-cutters and job-slashers[1]." I'm sorry, but I just don't buy that as a viable, strategy to transform business as usual into business at its best. Been there, done that, and it doesn't work if we truly want sustainable leadership, organizations and communities.

President Barack Obama's inaugural theme in 2009 was

"Renewing America's Promise;" regardless of political persuasions, we must all get about the business of renewing our promise – as leaders, as organizations and as communities. I sincerely hope that this book serves as a guide for living up to that promise and being the best we can be as effective, ethical and engaging leaders and institutions.

Do not believe in anything simply because you have heard it. Do not believe in anything simply because it is spoken and rumored by many. Do not believe in anything simply because it is found written in your religious books. Do not believe in anything merely on the authority of your teachers and elders. Do not believe in traditions because they have been handed down for many generations. But after observation and analysis, when you find that anything agrees with reason and is conducive to the good and benefit of one and all, then accept it and live up to it.
Buddha

It's not what we eat but what we digest that makes us strong; not what we gain but what we save that makes us rich; not what we read but what we remember that makes us learned; and not what we profess but what we practice that gives us integrity.
Francis Bacon

Readers are invited to complete the free self-report *Leadership Integrity Survey* at www.integro-inc.com When prompted, enter this code:

FreeLIS

inTEgro's *Leadership Integrity Survey* will give you a fix on how you are currently navigating *Identity, Authenticity, Alignment* and *Accountability,* along with suggestions for navigating them more effectively.

NOTES

Introduction

1. Webster's New World Collegiate Dictionary; IDG New World Books Worldwide, Cleveland, OH, 1999
2. Gardner, Howard. Responsibility At Work; Jossey-Bass, San Francisco, CA, 2007
3. Young, Stephen. Moral Capitalism; Berrett-Koehler, San Francisco, CA, 2003

Chapter 1

1. Webster's New World Collegiate Dictionary; IDG New World Books Worldwide, Cleveland, OH, 1999
2. Woolard, Chris. Walker Information, 2010
3. Bennis, Warren. On Becoming a Leader, 4th edition; Perseus Publishing, Cambridge, MA, 2009
4. Gallup Management Journal; October, 2006
5. Thompson, Michael C. The Congruent Life; Jossey-Bass, San Francisco, CA, 2000
6. Kolb, David. "Integrity, Advanced Professional Development and Learning," in Executive Integrity (Suresh Srivasta and Associates. Jossey-Bass Publishers, San Francisco, CA, 1988)
7. Collins, James C. and Jerry Porras. Built To Last; Harper Business, New York, NY, 1994
8. Matoon, Mary Ann. Jungian Psychology in Perspective; The Free Press, New York, NY, 1981

Chapter 2

1. Cicero. De Officiis, I, xxx, 107, trans. Harry Edinger; Bobs-Merrill, Indianapolis, IN, 1974
2. Covey, Stephen R. The 7 Habits of Highly Effective

People; Fireside Press, New York, NY, 1989

3. Fulford, Robert. The Triumph of Narrative; Anansi, Toronto, ON, 1999

4. Whyte, David. Crossing the Unknown Sea – Work as a Pilgrimage of Identity; Riverhead Books, New York, NY, 2001

5. Hillman, James. The Soul's Code; Random House, New York, NY, 1996

6. Collins, Jim and Jerry Porras. Built To Last; Harper Business, New York, NY, 1994

7. McNally, David and Karl D. Speak. Be Your Own Brand; Barrett-Koehler Publishers, San Francisco, CA, 2002

8. Consulting Psychologists Press. www.cpp.com

9. Markopolis, Harry. No One Would Listen; John Wiley and Sons, New York, NY, 2010

10. Cohan, William. House of Cards; Random House, New York, NY, 2009

11. Ward, Vicky. The Devil's Casino; Wiley, New York, NY, 2010

12. Leider, Richard. The Power of Purpose; Ballantine Books, New York, NY, 1985

Chapter 3

1. SEED Magazine. Vol 2, No. 9; March, 2007, SEED Media Group, New York, NY

2. Parker, Palmer J. A Hidden Wholeness – The Journey Toward An Undivided Life; Jossey-Bass, San Francisco, CA, 2004

3. O'Donahue, John. Anam Cara; Harper Perennial, New York, NY, 2004. p 25

Chapter 4

1. Artwork by Lawrence Weiner, 1991
2. Mortenson, Greg. Was There A Loan It Didn't Like? New York Times; November 2, 2008
3. Labovitz, George and Victor Rosansky. The Power of Alignment; John Wiley and Sons, New York, NY, 1997
4. Foley, John. Balanced Brand; Jossey-Bass, San Francisco, CA, 2006,
5. George, Bill. Authentic Leadership; Jossey-Bass, San Francisco, CA, 2003
6. Senge, Peter. The Fifth Discipline; Doubleday, New York, NY, 1990
7. Collins, Jim. Good To Great; Harper Business, New York, NY, 2001
8. Goleman, Daniel. Working With Emotional Intelligence; Bantam Books, New York, NY, 1998
9. "The Global Leadership Imperative." Mercer Delta Executive Learning Center, 2006

Chapter 5

1. Connors, Roger, Tom Smith and Craig Hickman. The Oz Principle; Prentice Hall Press, Paramus, NJ, 1994
2. Kaplan, Roberts and David P. Norton. The Balanced Scorecard; Harvard Business School Press, Boston, MA, 1996
3. Musashi, Myamoto. A Book of Five Rings, translated by Victor Harris; Overlook Press, Woodstock, NY, 1974

Chapter 6

1. Covey, Stephen R. First Things First; Simon & Schuster, New York, NY, 1994

2. Goleman, Daniel. Working With Emotional Intelligence; Bantam Books, New York, NY, 1998
3. Lennick, Doug and Fred Kiel, PhD. Moral Intelligence; Wharton School Publishing, Upper Saddle River, NJ, 2005
4. The Benedictine Rule of Saint Benedict; Vintage, New York, NY, 1998

Parting Words
1. "Up The Ladder Step By Step," a review in the November 26, 2008 Wall Street Journal of "There's No Elevator To The Top" by Umesh Ramakrishnan. Portfolio / Penguin Publishing; New York, NY, 2008

INDEX

A

B

C

D

House of Cards 42

I

IBM 80

Identity challenge 23, 24, 39, 49, 52, 59, 61–62, 64, 125, 137

J

James, William v

Jobs, Steve 80

Johnson & Johnson 67, 124

Jung, Carl 15, 20, 40

K

Kaplan and Norton 126

Kiel, Fred 140

Kolb, David 18

Krispy Kreme 65, 66

L

Leader as Servant, The 91

Leadership And Organizational Integrity Model, viii, ix

Leadership Integrity Survey x, 171

Legend of Baggar Vance, The 64

Lehman Brothers 42, 50, 88, 139

Leider, Richard 48, 49

Lennick, Doug 140

listening 77, 104, 121, 156, 158, 159

M

W

Wachovia 50

Walker Information 13

Wall Street Journal 65

Wal-Mart 103

wholeness 15, 17, 111–112, 126, 129

Whyte, David 26

Wilson, Larry vii

WorldCom 162

Y

Young, Steven v

ABOUT THE AUTHOR

Al Watts is a veteran consultant. After ten years in private industry, Mr. Watts served leaders and their organizations for nearly thirty years as a resource for strategic planning, leadership and team coaching, organization assessment and development, and facilitation of complex meetings. Clients range across all sizes of publicly and privately held corporations, all government sectors and not-for-profits.

Mr. Watts is the founder of inTEgro, Inc, a practice that is committed to helping leaders and their organizations transform "business as usual" into business at its best. You can learn more about Al and inTEgro by visiting www.integro-inc.com.